2/2005

To Amy:

Hope This Book
Brings A

"Smile"

PLAYBILL®s
AND
POPCORN

PLAYBILL®S AND POPCORN

True Tales of Theatre, Tourism and Travel

Michael A. Jenkins

EAKIN PRESS ◆ Austin, Texas

We gratefully acknowledge the permission granted by Playbill, Incorporated for the use of their Registered Trademark.

Dedication

After my father, Wendell H. Jenkins, was killed in his airplane at an early age, I was raised by three women: my mother, Berniece M. Jenkins; my grandmother, Dora L. Pollard; and my aunt, Lucille D. Pollard. All taught and influenced me to respect others, but my mother is the one who gave me vision—opening my eyes to future possibilities and opportunities.

To my loving wife, Wendy, who gives me strength, inspiration, and encouragement every day.

To my children—Delanie, Angus, and Tiffany—who continually encourage me to never grow up.

And, to my granddaughter, Lila Grace—"I hope all your days are circus days."

ontents

Foreword by Jimmy Nederlander   vii
Acknowledgments   ix
Introduction: We're Off To Be the Wizard   1

  1. Curtain Up.   15
  2. Impossible Things Are Happening
     Every Day   31
  3. Dragon Tales   47
  4. On the Road Again and Again
     and Again   63
  5. Star Tales.   76
  6. Taking Nigeria for a Few Rides   95
  7. Up, Up and Awry   106
  8. Worlds of Fun.   117
  9. Tough Acts to Follow.   141
 10. Adventures Down Under   152
 11. Be My Guest   163
 12. Roadside Attractions   180

Afterword.   195
Awards.   199
Associations   201
Broadway and National Tours   203
Musicals Produced and/or Presented in Dallas . .   205
LARC Project List.   212
Musical Theatre Glossary   241
Index   245

Michael Jenkins with theatre impresario Jimmy Nederlander.

Foreword

The theatre business is beyond dog-eat-dog. It's shark-maul-shark—relentless and all-consuming.

Years ago, I watched a cherub-faced nice guy from Dallas plunge headlong into this shark-infested maelstrom. Ever since, Michael Jenkins has been swimming along, smiling his inscrutable little smile, surprising even the most fearsome of sharks.

He has the organizational skills of a commanding officer, the intuition of a soothsayer, the resourcefulness of a quarterback, and the fortitude of a lion tamer—which is a good thing, because in the theatre, there are a lot of lions, and a lot of mice who think they're lions.

Michael's not your everyday impresario. There's no bluster, no flamboyance, no "Look at me!" He's quiet and thoughtful—although he can be a bulldozer when he has to be. He gets things done, and he makes tough choices. But through it all, he's a gentleman. (Takes one to know one.)

Michael, of course, has another life beyond the theatre, running Leisure and Recreation Concepts, Inc., a theme park business. That makes all the sense in the world, because the theatre life, too, is one big roller coaster ride. You chug slowly, slowly upward, feeling at any moment as though you'll fall off the edge of the world. But then you crest that hill and *wheeeeeeee*—it's all downhill, and great fun.

These stories show the sort of life you have to live to be Michael Jenkins. There are endless rewards, but there are also moments of downright stupefaction. The ride can leave you breathless, exhausted, and exhilarated, but it's never dull.

You want to talk about multi-tasking? Michael Jenkins is the ultimate juggler. Read these stories and see. At any moment, he's got several dozen balls in play. He knows one could drop at any moment, but he's not afraid to take that risk.

A lot of people fail because they forget about the "business" end of theatre business. But Michael, nice guy that he is, also keeps his eye on the bottom line. He always has his game face on. And his game face isn't a glower or grimace. It's this cryptic little grin, like he knows something the rest of us don't. Maybe he does.

JIMMY NEDERLANDER

Acknowledgments

To Helen Bryant and John Anders for their untiring efforts in encouraging me to write these stories and for making the stories readable.

To the Eakin Press staff–Melissa Roberts, Virginia Messer, and Pat Molenaar–for their expertise.

To my two long-time assistants–Wanda Beth for helping me remember the stories, record them, and proof the early drafts, and to Jenny Cagle for her assistance in gathering data.

A special thank you to my wife, Wendy, for her encouragement, patience, and long hours devoted to selecting the title for this book based on the theatre and tourism industries.

And, especially, to all of the individuals and real life "characters" I have encountered, in addition to the performers, actors, actresses, land developers, and entrepreneurs who live the stories you are about to read.

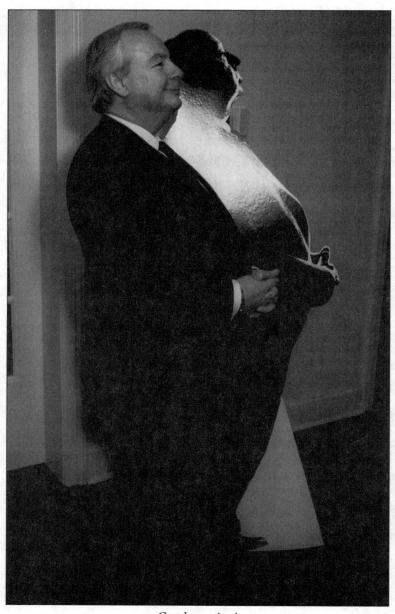

Good evening!

INTRODUCTION:

We're Off To Be the Wizard

I've always loved putting on a show.

But I've always preferred to be the man behind the curtain—and the man behind the midway—rather than the guy who stands out front and takes the bows. I'm more comfortable behind the scenes.

As you'll learn in the coming chapters, I did take a few turns on the stage. As a child in Dallas, Texas, I was cast in a production of *The Pied Piper*. I was chosen for the role of a rat—perhaps because of my superb scampering ability; I'd hate to think it was typecasting. What started as an on-stage role soon became an off-stage one. But more about that later.

I got my first real show-business job while I was in high school. I painted numbers on seats in the Cotton Bowl in Fair Park. I quickly appreciated just how many seats there were—and the importance of putting posteriors in them.

Then I took a job at the Music Hall at Fair Park.

Another kid named Tom Hughes and I assisted the manager, Charles Meeker, with various duties. Tom and I would both wind up running Dallas Summer Musicals, one after the other, but at that point in our careers, we were just happy to be doing any sort of work in a real, live theatre.

There were perks, of course. One of them was occasionally running into a star. Maurice Chevalier was one of them. He was earning, at the time, the most money that Dallas Summer Musicals had ever paid a performer: $100,000 for a week of shows. We started the shows on Monday instead of the usual Tuesday to squeeze in an extra performance.

Mr. Chevalier was a very polite man, but very nervous. Before each performance, he'd

Above: *Bunny.*
Below: *Indian.*

2

Above: *Clowning around.*
Below: *Piggy.*

walk along the fence of the Texas State Fairgrounds, near the Music Hall, to calm his butterflies.

I remember that when he performed at the Music Hall, management wanted to turn off the lights and lock the doors after the performance started, so he wouldn't be interrupted or distracted. But Mr. Chevalier said no—leave the doors open.

"But Mr. Chevalier," I protested, "that will ruin your opening number."

He sat me down and explained that some of the people in the audience had saved up to buy tickets and had come a long way to see him.

"It's the audience that matters," he said. "I want to have the opportunity to perform for them. Without them, I am nothing." I've always held on to that thought.

When it came time

3

for college, I wanted to study theatre at the University of Southern California. But, being an only child, my mother did not want me to go that far away from home since my father had been killed in a private plane crash. My mother, Berniece, wanted me to accept an architecture scholarship to Texas A&M.

So, we compromised. I went to Baylor University, where I studied theatre management and produced shows, on and off campus. My mother wasn't thrilled. She hadn't seen a whole lot of ads in the "help wanted" section for theatre managers.

I promised her: I'll get a job.

After college, I took a job at Six Flags Over Texas in Arlington, where Angus G. Wynne, Jr., the founder of Six Flags, taught me so much about making audiences happy that I'd eventually name my son after him. I was in awe of the man.

His inspiration, along with Walt Disney's, led me to eventually open my own business for creating, developing, and managing amusement parks worldwide—Leisure and Recreation Concepts. It's a good name, with an appropriate acronym—LARC. Our objective is to make life a lark for all those who visit our parks. It certainly isn't always a lark for us, but it's been interesting.

In the amusement park business, everything's a three-ring circus. What can you say about a job that involves having to truck in sand to build an amusement park in a desert? About a job that lets you create the very first amusement park ever in Nigeria? About a job building the very first miniature golf course in China?

What we did in some of these countries brought smiles to people's faces in ways they'd never experienced. You haven't lived until you've seen a father of a large family staring, wide-eyed, at a Ferris wheel for the first time.

My son, Angus, is my right-hand man at LARC. In fact, sometimes I think I'm his right hand; he's always coming up with new ideas for marketing and improving our work.

I remember going to Angus' soccer games, when he was little, with my cell phone. I'd be talking to somebody on the other side of the world, but I'd be cheering Angus at the same time. I got him a customized

Angus Jenkins, Michael's son, is his right hand at LARC, Inc.

bumper car from an amusement park to tool around the neighborhood in. He really liked that. So I guess he figured the amusement park business wasn't so bad.

This sort of work can't help but be exciting—and exhausting. You have to wake up excited about it. It's something new every day. We carry the mood into our office, which has a popcorn machine in the conference room and a sign that can be hand-lettered daily to welcome whoever is coming into our conference room.

So I had plenty to do before I took on the job of running Dallas Summer Musicals. It all happened very fast, and I really didn't have time to think about how I'd find time to do the work.

I'd been a big fan of Dallas Summer Musicals for some time and had, of course, known Tom Hughes, its managing director, since childhood. Tom had done a good job with the musicals, but in the early '90s he became ill, and as a result things weren't going so well for the musicals.

When Tom died, after an interim director held it together briefly, I was hired—in a hurry—because the operation was foundering badly. It was 1994, and the musicals were in turmoil. Union contracts had been allowed to expire, and subscriptions were down to 8,700. There were a lot of people who thought Dallas Summer Musicals wouldn't live another year.

I had to put together my first season at roughly the speed of light. I realized that marketing would be the key to making that 1995 season work, so I threw a lot of effort that way, and it paid off.

Show business is about putting on a show and running a business. We try to walk a fine line between the business side and the creative side. Most of the time, it works.

Season subscriptions are now 30,000, with packed houses. We now have a full-time, year-round staff of fifty; there were only three people in 1994.

I've been able to work a lot of my amusement park business knowledge into the theatre business, too. Just one example: I noticed a lot of Music Hall guests had to park several blocks away and trudge all the way back to the Music Hall. So I invested in a tram for them to ride. They seem to like it.

Now, as president and managing director of Dallas Summer Musicals, I've become accustomed to wrangling with actors and the baggage they bring (Jerry Lewis showed up with forty-four trunks, but that's not

Jerry Lewis gets some laughs at a Dallas Summer Musicals press conference.

the kind of baggage I'm talking about). I'm used to head-butting with unions and giant media production companies. And I'm always focused on making sure every single person in the audience is totally happy—even when his or her demands are completely ridiculous. The customer may not always be right, but he's always the customer.

In 1998, I added management of The Majestic Theatre to the Dallas Summer Musicals plate. That big, beautiful hall wasn't being used to its potential; it was booked only 16 percent of the time. Now we have it booked 83 percent of the time. And the shows we offer there in our Broadway Contemporary Series are edgier than the ones our Dallas Summer Musicals subscribers might want. With these new shows, we're able to draw more young people into the theatre.

I've learned that the theatre business is a big pond, and little fish have to form a school in order to have any muscle. So I organized theatre companies around the country into a consortium, so that we could coordinate touring shows. That way, I can buy twenty weeks of a show, instead of just two weeks for Dallas, and I have more negotiating power with major tour producers. I like to say that we used to be tied up and gagged in the trunk of the car. We don't always drive now, but at least we get to ride in the front seat.

In recent years I've learned that there's more truth in that musical comedy *The Producers* than anyone could have guessed. Dallas Summer Musicals and I have become investors in Broadway shows, including *Thoroughly Modern Millie*, *The King and I*, *Big River*, and *Flower Drum Song*, which we produced ourselves. We've invested in 120 shows—Broadway, off-Broadway

8

and touring—and most of them have been money-makers.

Putting my own money where my mouth is has taught me to pay even more attention to the vagaries of audience tastes. It's scary, but I like it. High risks carry high rewards. My friend Benjamin Mordecai, with whom I've produced several shows, says it's an advantage that I'm not a New York guy. I see things from a different perspective.

Michael Jenkins with Flower Drum Song *and* Miss Saigon *star Lea Solonga.*

The Majestic Theatre, where Michael Jenkins produces the Broadway Contemporary Series for Dallas Summer Musicals.

We've also opened a school at Dallas Summer Musicals to develop young talent. More than 750 students have gone through the program. I've had a lot of the kids and their parents thank me, but really, I'm the one who should thank them. They're the stars of tomorrow. When we're negotiating contracts someday for a show I'm producing, I hope they remember me.

Yes, all this is a lot of work, but I like work. And theatre and amusement parks have a lot in common, when you get right down to it. It's all one great, big, fun ride; you just have to be careful not to fall off.

Speaking of rides: Between the shows and the amusement parks, I find I spend a great deal of my life on airplanes. In fact, my favorite expression is, "Talk

Michael Jenkins and colleagues listen intently at Dallas Summer Musicals auditions.

fast—I'm late for the plane." If getting there isn't half the fun, it's at least half the adventure. You wouldn't believe some of the things that happen at 30,000 feet. But you're about to find out.

Somehow, between shows and amusement parks and all those air-

Michael and Wendy Jenkins enjoy a dance.

plane rides, I managed to find the love of my life, Wendy. I found her in Georgia, where she was promoting tourism for a little gold-rush town called Dahlonega.

Of course, our courtship had to be a major production. I was always sending her things. One time I sent 100 roses to her office. Wendy says every man in town hated me after that. Another time, I sent a big box of fortune cookies. Each one had the same fortune in it: "Rest up! Big Tex is on his way!"

It worked. She married me. And she works with me now, too, at LARC and by my side at the Music Hall. Her smile keeps the lights burning on my personal stage.

How does a guy simultaneously run a theatre business and an amusement park business and have some semblance of a life? Carefully. It's a life on the high wire, and it's all about balance.

Michael Jenkins with his mother, wife, and son.

Michael, Mickey Mouse and Tiffany (daughter) at Disneyland.

Michael's daughters, Delanie and Tiffany.

Delanie with her daughter, Lila.

CHAPTER ONE:

#

ACT ONE: I AM A RAT

I never dreamed, when I was a child, that I'd have a career in the theatre. All I knew, during one year at Lida Hooe Elementary School in North Oak Cliff, was that I wanted desperately to play the role of a rat in our production of *The Pied Piper*.

I have no idea why I preferred the role of a rodent to that of the Pied Piper, but I did. Happily, I was selected.

My grandmother, who was a wonderful seamstress, made my rat costume, and I was extremely proud of it.

My part was to crawl between the legs of the choir while they were singing and to then crawl out onto the stage, only to be wooed off-stage later by the Pied Piper.

As I crawled between the legs of the choir members, I began looking desperately to find my mother in the audience. This was my first performance, after all.

As I crawled forward, simultaneously searching the

15

seats for my mother, I found myself without any more stage to crawl on. I fell off the stage, onto the piano, and into the lap of the pianist, who also happened to be the director of the production. Obviously, this was one rat that didn't follow the Pied Piper.

This should've ended my career in theatre. It didn't. But it did end my desire to be a rat.

LET'S RUN ME UP THE FLAGPOLE AND SEE WHO SALUTES

I also had a starring role every morning in my elementary school's front yard. I was very proud to have been selected to raise the American flag each day. I would bring it out from the office, attach it to the rope with two clips, and pull it very evenly and strategically to the top.

As I looked at the top of that pole every morning, I thought, if only I could climb to the top of that pole, I would be able to see the world.

So, one morning I decided to do just that. I attached the flag to the top of the two clips on the pole and my blue jean belt loop to the sec-

Flag Mike

16

ond clip. As I hoisted the flag, I also hoisted myself. What a feeling!

I was on my way to the top. I would be able to see the world.

But then, about a third of the way up, my belt loop snapped and I went tumbling to the ground, landing in a freshly watered flower bed. It wasn't the mud that upset me as much as that rope spinning out of control, finally landing in a heap beside me. My mother had to get the fire department to come out and put a new rope on the flagpole.

My days of putting up the flag were over.

THE FIRST DINNER THEATRE

I like to point out that in order to be in show business, you have to love shows, but you also have to know business.

This is another lesson I learned in elementary school.

I was one of the boys trained to operate the projection equipment in what was called the "flicker room," the room where students came to watch educational films.

One day as I was walking home from school—I always chose the alleys because they were so much more interesting than the main streets—I found a roll of film. Not knowing exactly what it was, I took it home and held it, frame by frame, up to the light.

To my great joy, it turned out to be a "Felix the Cat" film.

The next day, I took it to school, and during lunch

17

hour I went upstairs to the film room and put it in the projector. It was a delightful cartoon.

The wheels in my head began to turn. There were approximately 200 children who ate lunch in the lunchroom at the same time every day, then went outside to play on the playground when they were finished.

On the second day, I quietly circulated word that I was in possession of a "Felix the Cat" cartoon that I would show at lunch time for five cents a person. The nickels rolled in.

The third day, I figured out the value of concessions. On my way to school, I dropped by the 7-Eleven of my day and purchased some candy, which I resold at a slight markup to moviegoers. It seemed these kids would never tire of watching the wonderful, wonderful cat at lunch time.

By the end of the week, though, the teachers were wondering why the playground was virtually bare after lunch. Where had everyone gone?

It was discovered that I had a packed house in the film room. By then, I had

Cub Scout Mike

18

made—including candy sales—almost $11, and I was very proud of myself.

The school and my mother, of course, felt that my entrepreneurial spirit was inappropriate during school lunches. My mother made me give the $11 to the PTA. But at that point, I knew there was no business like show business. I was hooked for life.

THE HOUSE OF USHER

My first job was as an usher at the Music Hall at Fair Park, working for Charles Meeker, the original producer of the Dallas Summer Musicals. He was, of course, a grand impresario and flamboyant figure—a true mentor to me, although I've never been accused of being flamboyant, come to think of it.

Anyway, I think Charlie felt sorry for me and wanted to give me a daytime job. The Summer Musicals were in the evening, of course. So during the daytime, I was assigned to paint numbers on all the seats in the Cotton Bowl.

Think of it: 75,504 seats. It took me all summer long to paint those numbers at 35 cents an hour. I spent the better part of a full day just figuring out how much I would earn that summer.

It was not unusual for people to try to break into the Cotton Bowl or even jump over the fence for an important event that was to transpire later (Rolling Stones concert, Texas-Oklahoma football game, etc.). So, Charlie Meeker would lock me in and come back to get me that evening at the Cotton Bowl.

One day he was downtown in a hectic meeting and

19

couldn't get back to let me out. I waited a long time to be released from this cavernous prison, but Charlie never came.

I'm probably the only person who ever climbed that tall fence to get *out* of the Cotton Bowl.

A FLASH OF BRILLIANCE

Rules are made to be broken. The difference between a kid and a grownup is knowing when to break them.

One of my first assignments at the Music Hall at Fair Park, aside from being an usher and painting numbers on the seats at the Cotton Bowl, was a task assigned to me by Charles Meeker, director of the Music Hall from 1945 to 1960.

I was to go around closing and locking all the doors in the Music Hall when the Dallas Symphony was getting ready to rehearse. In those days, the symphony performed in the Music Hall.

On one particular day, I was closing the doors so that the symphony could rehearse with violinist Fritz Kreisler. Mr. Kreisler had made clear that if anyone came in and took a flash picture of him during rehearsal, he would refuse to perform.

So, I made sure the doors were secure. I was the only soul in the 4,216 seats the hall had at that time. I was enjoying the rehearsal when I spotted, out of the corner of my eye, a little boy of about nine climbing out of the orchestra pit, a Brownie Hawkeye flash camera around his neck.

Yikes!

I ran down the aisle so fast that my feet got ahead of me and I almost fell. I grabbed the young man by the collar of his coat, marched him out of the auditorium, and deposited him outside in the November chill. Dusting off my hands, I locked the door, knowing I had done a great job.

At the conclusion of the rehearsal, Mr. Meeker was on-stage talking with Mr. Kreisler, who had an irritated look on his face. Mr. Meeker, looking very concerned, motioned for me to come forward.

"Have you seen Mr. Kreisler's grandson?" he asked.

Oops.

He's not going to quit his day job, but Michael Jenkins got to conduct the overture to My Fair Lady *at one performance.*

A DARK SENSE OF HUMOR

Creative problem-solving is a big part of the entertainment and tourism industries—because there are plenty of problems to solve.

I remember one of my early attempts at creative problem solving. I was taking a world history class at Baylor University, and the professor instructed us to spend six weeks developing an intricate cartoon focusing on an important event in history. My classmates went right to work. I promptly forgot about the assignment—until the night before.

The problem I had to solve was this: I had to come up with a cartoon project that contained six weeks' worth of wonderful work—but I had to come up with it in one night. So I went to the drug store and bought some multicolored construction paper. I slipped a single sheet of black construction paper out of the packet and wrote my name on it, legibly.

The next morning, we all turned in our work. Everyone around me had produced intricate cartoons on such subjects as the Battle of Waterloo, festooned with hundreds of soldiers that had taken weeks to draw.

I turned in my black sheet of paper.

"What's this?" asked the professor.

"It's my cartoon," I announced.

"Huh?" he replied.

"It's the Dark Ages," I said.

All my classmates rolled their eyes in unison. But the professor was intrigued. He gave out only four A's on that assignment. I got one of them.

DRIVING THE BOSS CRAZY

It was on a pleasant Sunday that I scared my boss nearly to death on Interstate 30.

I was driving on I-30, then called the DFW Turnpike (it's the Tom Landry Freeway now) when I happened to drive up behind Angus Wynne, Jr., my boss at Six Flags Over Texas. I didn't know it at first; Mr. Wynne had a new car. But as he pulled to the outside lane, I recognized him and his wife, heading west, toward Six Flags.

I was happy to see him. I waved. In my exuberance, I accidentally steered into his lane, running him out of the lane and off the highway, into the dust.

I was mortified. Rather than stop and apologize, I did the rational thing—I panicked, floored it, and drove out of sight.

I hid out all afternoon, certain that I would be fired.

The next day, my secretary stuck her head in my office.

"He's coming down the hall," she announced. I knew he'd be bringing a pink slip. Indeed, he was carrying a piece of paper, which he'd had his secretary fill out. But I wasn't fired.

"I want you to get these personalized license plates on your car," he said, handing me the paper. "That way, I'll always know when you're coming." I got the plates and had them the rest of the time I was at Six Flags.

The plates read SFOT-MJ. That stood for Six Flags Over Texas—Michael Jenkins. Or maybe it was really Scary Fellow on the Turnpike—Michael Jenkins.

IN THE DRIVER'S SEAT

It's always a little unnerving when you're treated better than you think you should be. The question arises: Why? What do they know that I don't?

One day I was invited to the State Fair for a meeting. As I drove up to the gate to park, I was met by a motorcycle police officer who said he would escort me to the Fair's office.

Escort me he did, right down the Midway, past Big Tex. I was extremely embarrassed. I hate being the center of attention; I'm the backstage guy. Here were all these people walking, and I'm in a car, like some big shot. People were looking at me as though I must be, well, somebody.

Turns out the officer thought I was a big shot. It was those license plates: SFOT-MJ. He thought it stood for State Fair of Texas, and that I was somebody official. Is MJ short for maharajah? Angus Wynne, Jr., never knew what a favor he'd done me by insisting on those plates.

BA-A-A-A-D ACTING

In my early days at Six Flags one of my duties was to supervise Guest Relations—which is sometimes nothing more than a glamorous name for the complaint department.

On a Saturday evening, a lady came by our office with a hole in her dress. She said a goat in the children's petting zoo had taken a big bite out of her best dress, a precious family heirloom.

24

Yeah, right, the very sort of garment one wears to an amusement park. The dress, it turns out, was from J.C. Penney's wash and wear sun dress collection. So whaddya gonna do?

Because of the number of complaints an amusement park must process, our insurance company determined we could settle claims of $50 or less on our own judgment. So I offered her a check for fifty bucks, which was a pretty good amount of money in those days. She reluctantly accepted it, signed the waiver, and exited the park in a huff at about 9:30 on a Saturday evening.

The following morning I was back at the park in Guest Relations standing near a one-way window that looks out on the turnstiles. I happened to notice the same lady walking through the park entrance. And doggone if she wasn't wearing yet another family heirloom.

I followed her at a discreet distance directly to the petting zoo, where I found her holding out a wadded-up length of the back of her dress for the goat's perusal. Obviously, she was inviting the goat to take another big bite.

So I tapped her on the shoulder and asked, "May I help you?"

As she turned around, the first words out of her mouth were, "What are you doing here? You were working here last night."

I said, "Madam, I was here last night and I'm here again today, and we're not paying for another dress."

With great disappointment, she let go of the portion of her dress meant to tempt the goat and walked straight out of the park. I sort of wish she had taken the goat along with her. I was beginning to think the pair of them were in cahoots.

SCHOOL'S OUT

I'll tell you in a later chapter about Venezuelan federal troops stationed outside the zoo to keep renegade locals from climbing over the walls and killing the animals for food.

Who would imagine we'd have trouble at Six Flags keeping people from trying to climb out of the park. That became one of our big challenges when Six Flags began hosting all-night high-school graduation parties. We had to refuse to let anyone out of the park until the next morning because we didn't want the fellas sneaking out in the middle of the night with their girlfriends. It was for safety reasons and, well, you can imagine all sorts of scenarios.

I was amazed at the craftiness of these young people. It was always shocking to me how they tried to smuggle in all kinds of liquor and cigarettes, even cigars. Most of these items were strapped to the inside thighs of girlfriends, who were searched at the gates by parents and PTA members—not by our company.

Over the years we had people crossing the railroad tracks and climbing over the fences trying to get into the park. But that was nothing compared to the kids trying to scale the walls out of the park during those commencement parties. Graduation is not all pomp and circumstance.

THE SECOND ACT BEGINS

I was in Seville, Spain, working on a project in December of 1994 when I received a frazzled call from the chairman of the Dallas Summer Musicals. He had big problems.

The Musicals' managing director, Tom Hughes, had died, and not long afterward contracts had expired and everything was a mess.

The theatre's executive board—mainly doctors, lawyers, and Indian chiefs—admitted that theatre was not their bailiwick.

I never saw myself as a savior, but let's face it, I just love the Summer Musicals. The Musicals gave me one of my first jobs (house usher). And for former directors Charlie Meeker and Tom Hughes, I just couldn't let the tradition expire without a fight.

So my original intention was to attract new audiences and build—brick by brick—on the foundation left behind by Charlie and Tom.

Sometimes you need to grasp the small image before proceeding on to the Big Picture. One of the first things I did was to add security and better lighting to the parking lot. Whether the problems were real or perceived, Fair Park safety issues needed to be addressed. We also put red-jacketed attendants on duty to walk people to their cars, if desired.

And I made a deal with taxicab companies to have cars waiting after each performance. Hotels would not send people out to the Music Hall, because there were no taxis back then. We told the cabbies we'd give them $5 if they didn't get a pickup in fifteen minutes. I figured they might as well be sitting outside the Music Hall as someplace downtown.

These sorts of things just seemed logical to me. They were, in fact, the first baby steps in what was to be a long, wonderful—and yes, strange—journey.

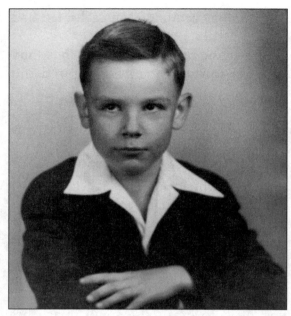

*Dapper even
in the early
years . . .*

*and forever
on the go.*

No, not running for office— but his platform is entertainment!

Michael and his mother, Berniece, at LARC's annual Christmas party.

Michael with granddaughter Lila.

CHAPTER TWO:

■■■ mpossible Things
☀ Are Happening
■■■ Every Day

THE GREAT FLOOD

Inside the Music Hall at Fair Park on May 5, 1995, Tommy Tune was dancing in *Stage Door Charley*, Dallas Summer Musical's opening show of the season. Outside the Music Hall, a horror show was playing— starring Mother Nature. And me.

For hours, the skies had gushed gallons, and a lake had formed in the Music Hall's parking lot, rising higher and higher.

As some of my staff watched from a window of the Music Hall, they saw a blue Cadillac float by. Inside the car, hands and feet glued to the window like one of those Garfield toys, was their boss—me. I'd gotten in the car to try to keep it from getting carried off by the rising water. But I'd failed miserably and was now being swept away, captive in a floating Caddy.

I had just weeks earlier been named managing

31

director of Dallas Summer Musicals, and I was beginning to wonder if I'd gotten in over my head. Trial
by fire I could handle. But this was trial by flood, and
I wasn't at all sure the verdict would be favorable.

The night had started normally enough. The audience of 2,192 had arrived. The show had started
on time. Then the deluge began. This was the sort of
rain that a city like Dallas—far from the tropics—rarely
sees. There were waves in the parking lot. Debris
had blocked a fence where water normally could have
escaped, so the area quickly filled with water.

Watching from the lobby, I saw a woman who had
fallen in the parking lot and went outside to help her.

I took my car, which was parked right next to the
Music Hall, drove around and located the lady, then
got out and opened my umbrella—which the wind immediately ripped apart. The lady, about seventy and
clearly terrified, said the wind and rain had blown her
down before she could get to her car. I tried to put her
in my car, but she was as scared of me as she was of
the weather. So I helped her into her own car, where
she sat soaked and trembling.

I told her I'd go get some towels from wardrobe,
but when I turned around, my car was on the move.
What the heck—did I forget to take it out of gear? I ran
and jumped in, realizing that the car was in "park" but
was being carried off by the water, now with me in it.

My car was immediately hit by another car and
spun around 360 degrees. I sailed on past the Music
Hall, hit by a number of other cars along the way. It
was at this point that staff in the Crystal Terrace, the
Music Hall's restaurant, saw me pass. Ahoy.

My car floated against the black iron gates at the

entrance to Fair Park, bounced off, and began to sink. I called the Music Hall on my cell phone to let them know what was up, but I didn't have long to chat. The water was rising in the car, the power windows wouldn't open, and I had about eleven inches between the water and the roof of my car. It was time to exit.

I braced myself against the steering wheel and the driver's seat and, with both feet, pushed the door and window out. I went tumbling into a strong current that carried me back toward the Music Hall, where I grabbed a crape myrtle tree. The limb broke, and off I went until I caught another tree. By that time, the Music Hall was an island, and I was doing my best to swim and claw my way back to it.

Finally, I made it, and the staff members who'd been watching me helped me into the building. I sloshed back to wardrobe to change clothes and put mine in the dryer.

Meanwhile, things were not going well inside. After a deafening thunderclap and flash of lightning, I saw sparks leap from the stage lighting computers. The lights flickered.

Tommy Tune had stopped dancing and was wringing his hands. He told the audience that something was amiss, and the lighting would need to be fixed. The show took a break to fix the lighting, then the show continued.

But at around 9:40 I got a phone call from a power company guy who imparted the news that of the seventeen electrical transformers in the area, eleven were under water, including some of the Music Hall's.

What, I asked, did this mean?

It meant, the power guy said, that within three to five minutes the transformers could explode and electrocute anyone in the water. He strongly suggested that within these three to five minutes we shut down the power at the Music Hall. Sounded like good advice to me.

So, I got my clothes out of the dryer (no, they weren't dry, but they fit me better than anything in wardrobe) and explained to the company manager that we were going to have to stop the show. He did a one-act tragedy about how unhappy the New York producers would be, noting that it would all be on my head. My head, with its sopping wet hair, agreed to take on the responsibility.

So, at the end of a musical number, I went on-stage and explained to the audience, in a this-happens-all-the-time-don't-worry tone, that the show was going to have to stop; the power was going out, and they would be plunged into blackness, but they could not leave the building and must stay seated until the independent generator restored limited power.

Meanwhile, water was pouring in through the stage doors, and the orchestra pit was becoming a swimming pool. All forty-nine cars in the staff parking lot were afloat, some upside down. The good news: We'd managed to cut the power before the transformers blew and electrocuted anybody.

The audience was taking all this very well, sipping drinks in the restaurant (we'd asked the waiters to lock up all the liquor so that drunken brawls wouldn't be added to our list of woes). Tommy Tune was kind enough to visit with people, and I promised—and provided—updates on the situation every fifteen minutes.

By 1:30 A.M., the waves in the parking lot had re-
ceded to a slight chop, and those audience members
whose cars would run were allowed to drive away, led
by police cars. About two-thirds of the cars in the
upper parking lot qualified for the convoy. The other
third—and almost all the cars in the lower lot—were
under water—269 cars total.

By 2:00 A.M., we were able to get city buses to the
Music Hall, and we organized the audience members
into destination groups—one for Plano, one for Fort
Worth, etc.—and feeling very much like Noah, I led the

*After cars were trashed in a Dallas rainstorm at the Music Hall at
Fair Park, Michael Jenkins arranged for everybody to be bused home.*

patrons to their buses, which dropped them off as close to their homes as possible. Ushers and staff—except for a few key people and, of course, me—went home on those buses, too.

While a crew mopped up the Music Hall, my son, Angus, who had been with me at the Music Hall, took me home to change clothes and get a rental car. When I got back at 6:30 A.M., I noticed a wrecker moving a pickup truck so he could get to another car. Odd, I thought. I asked security to investigate.

Turns out this guy with the wrecker was stealing a car—as he had a couple of others during the night. To keep this from happening again, I got the city to agree to tow the cars to a safe place and not charge their owners anything.

Oh, and we had a show to do that afternoon. And it WAS going on, because we couldn't afford to lose another performance. The power was back, and somehow we got everything dried out, except for a few rows of seats, whose ticket-holders were reassigned to comparable dry areas. Whew.

The Music Hall, happily, got past this stormy season opening.

Stage Door Charley didn't fare so well. Tommy Tune broke his foot a few months later, and the show died without making it to Broadway.

LIGHTS OUT

In the middle of an executive committee meeting for Dallas Summer Musicals, I receive an urgent call: *The Sound of Music*, twelve minutes into its second act of

36

its Thursday matinee, had no sound of music. No lights, either. The power had gone out.

Rushing back to the Music Hall, I grabbed a battery-powered bullhorn and went on-stage to direct the audience out of the pitch-black theatre. As they departed, I promised to bring them back to another performance, even though we had only four performances left and all were virtually sold out. I'd work it all out later, I figured.

The blackout, it turned out, was most likely caused by a freak power surge at the city bus maintenance facility. The surge sent power backward through the lines, knocking out transformers at the Music Hall and other Fair Park buildings. It also burned up eleven main breakers and burned the cable and back-up transformer, which then fell on the backup generator. The odds of all this happening are probably higher than those of winning the Texas Lottery, but that's what happened. A lot of rewiring had to be done very quickly, but Texas Utilities came through for us, and we were back in business by noon the next day.

But in the meantime, we had lost not only the Thursday matinee but also the Thursday night performance. To accommodate all those people from the audiences, we would clearly have to add another performance. Would the unions help defray the cost? They would not. It wasn't an act of God, they said: It was an act of electricity. So we paid the cost of adding a performance.

You should know, though, that the new wiring installed that night is more than an inch and a half thick and should last a nice, long time.

IF THE SLIPPER FITS

"Impossible things are happening every day!"

It's probably the fairy godmother's best-known line from *Cinderella*, and it's true.

I wish I'd been there to see the following episode, but I heard about it in a letter from Georgia Engel, who starred as the fairy godmother in our touring production of *Cinderella*. Georgia is probably best remembered as Georgette (Ted Baxter's wife) on the Mary Tyler Moore Show. She's a stitch.

Georgia had played the fairy godmother in Dallas, and everyone loved her. As I noted earlier, my first year at Dallas Summer Musicals was pretty harried, to say the least. But our production of *Cinderella* went like clockwork.

Apparently, it was an entirely different story at Kansas City, where the show traveled immediately after Dallas. The show was mounted at the Kansas City Starlight Theatre, an outdoor facility, and in Kansas City's production, I suggested they might want to use a couple of real Shetland ponies on-stage with Cinderella's coach. I also agreed when I was asked if they could employ some unspecified special effects. I must have been asleep when I made that phone call. Never agree to a special effect when you don't know what that effect—or its aftereffects—will be. As for horses, never use a live horse when a stuffed one will suffice. These were lessons this production would teach me.

The Kansas City cast had performed a walk-through of the carriage scene but never managed a full rehearsal. Everything had gone so well in Dallas. Why bother?

Eartha Kitt and Michael Jenkins stand in front of the Cinderella *carriage.*

So there they were, during the opening night production, with Cinderella about to step into the carriage as the first act ends. Time for the special effects: sparklers and roman candles, set to go off as the fairy godmother utters her famous line. Only they didn't tell Georgia about the fireworks. And they didn't know she's deathly afraid of all explosives.

So, as the carriage pulled up, and Georgia declaimed, "Impossible things are happening every day!" the sparklers went off right next to her. Unfortunately the fireworks were studded with too much firepower.

And Georgia fainted dead away.

The horses spooked, too. (They were huge Clydesdales, not the shetland ponies I'd recommended.) They reared up on stage before tearing off like racing thoroughbreds at the starting gate. At this point, poor Cinderella had not yet stepped into her carriage. When the horses panicked, she instinctively grabbed the door handle of the carriage with both hands.

Cinderella hung on for dear life while the horses dragged her off-stage at full gallop.

As the Kansas City newspaper put it in its review of the production: "It's a shame Cinderella wasn't a rodeo rider. They only have to hold on for eight seconds."

IT *IS* UNUSUAL

Hollywood's all about image and legend. Truth sometimes works its way into the equation, but there's no obligation for it to do so. Just as many times, legend is just legend, and image is just image. It works just fine in Hollywood.

Take Tom Jones' cigarette lighter. (Please.)

Some years ago, when I was flying to California on a fairly regular basis, I went to the Sid and Marty Krofft Puppet Factory. It's run by two brothers, who produce marionette shows in which the marionettes are three and four feet high. At this point, they were working on a circus puppet and marionette show for Six Flags Over Texas, where I was working at the time.

I arrived at the airport and was picked up, true to Hollywood style, in a Rolls Royce. While we were driving to their Hollywood studio, I noticed that next to me in the back of the car, there was a gold cigarette lighter. On it were inscribed the initials "T. J." I assumed someone had accidentally left it in the car, and when I arrived in the office to see Marty Krofft, I pulled the lighter out and said, "I found this lighter in the Rolls. Somebody must have left it there."

"Oh," he said with practiced nonchalance, "that was Tom Jones. He was in the car last night."

I was impressed, of course. I thought no more about it until I was back in the puppet shop and one of the shop supervisors, Pat Quinn, asked me when I had arrived. I said I'd come in that morning, and the Rolls had brought me straight to the office.

"Did you find the gold lighter?" he asked.

"Yeah," I said. "It was Tom Jones'."

Pat chuckled. "Oh, they say that to everyone. They don't even know Tom Jones. They just keep this lighter in the car, and that's just part of the Hollywood scene."

Yeah, well. Tom Jones probably has a lighter in his Rolls with "M.K." on it. Nobody knows how to pull strings like Marty.

BETWEEN HEAVEN AND HELL

As everyone who means well knows, no good deed goes unpunished.

We had just completed remodeling the basement of The Majestic Theatre. It had been a storage room. We'd made it into a small experimental theatre that would hold between 80 and 140 people, depending on how the seats were configured. We actually built this theatre as an incubator for small theatre groups that could not afford to use the Majestic but whom we wanted to encourage until they grew successful enough to move to larger stages.

One morning I read in the paper that a small theatre group's performing space had caught on fire and burned down. I called and offered them the new space if they'd like to use it temporarily, until their theatre was rebuilt.

They were delighted and asked if they could immediately put on their annual production. I agreed—unfortunately, without asking what it was.

They moved into the theatre within a week, and everything was going well until one day, about three weeks later, when I received an urgent call from the cultural affairs division of the City of Dallas. They informed me that there was a problem in The Majestic Theatre that I needed to look into.

OK, I said.

No, they said: This needs your attention RIGHT NOW.

I dropped what I was doing and went down to the Majestic, where I found this situation percolating unhappily: A religious group had booked the main theatre with a production of *Coming to the Lord*. The group I'd given the basement to had a big sign in the lobby announcing its production: *The Devil's Going to Get You*.

To put it mildly, the Christians were displeased.

We were able to find a suitable location for the sign promoting *The Devil's Going to Get You* outside the theatre, where it could point the way to that production (down, of course) without interfering with the sensibilities of those headed upward.

42

AND YOUR LITTLE DOG, TOO

It was on the way to the first rehearsal of our production of *The Wizard of Oz* that I realized that in putting together the cast, costumes, and sets for this show, we'd forgotten one little thing: Toto. We had no dog.

We had to have a dog.

So, we went to the SPCA and found a dog that looked a bit like what we figured Toto looked like. But I was concerned that this dog, of unknown heritage, might not be able to learn its lines and blocking in the short time before the show opened. Training an animal usually takes time.

I called an animal trainer friend, and he said I had no problem. All you do is smear some frankfurters on the stage where you want the dog to be. In a short time, the dog will be able to follow that. And, he said, give a few frankfurters to Dorothy, too. She'll keep them in her pocket, and the dog will follow her.

Sounded good. We bought the frankfurters, the dog was wonderful, and everything worked the way it was supposed to, except for one thing. The dog didn't like Dorothy. He loved the Wicked Witch.

When the witch would come into Dorothy's farmhouse to take Toto and put him in the basket and take him away, the dog couldn't wait to go. He snarled at Dorothy. He would actually run and eagerly jump into the witch's basket, smiling, with his tongue hanging out, waiting for the witch to take him away.

There really was no solution to this problem; we just had to let the dog have his way. He was so very fond of the witch.

Michael Jenkins loves meeting the actors and actresses who show up on tour—and Toto, too!

There was a raffle for the dog among cast members when the show was over. He probably was hoping the witch would win, but he did OK: One of the most beautiful and talented girls in the chorus won, and the dog is now living a happy life with her. He's retired from acting, though. Just couldn't stay in character.

NO LYIN'; THAT'S A LION

Everybody loves the circus. I always have. When I was growing up, my aunt always took us to the circus. We never missed a year. I'd remind her the circus was coming to town, and she'd get tickets and we'd go to the circus on Sunday afternoons.

Of course, coming home she spent half the time cleaning cotton candy off me so I'd be presentable when I got back.

I've kept up with the circus and, because I'm in the entertainment business, I've met some of the major players, such as John Ringling. I attended the circus with Kenneth Feld, current owner and producer of Ringling Bros. & Barnum and Bailey, and his wife, Bonnie, at the American Airlines Arena in Dallas.

So I pass up no opportunity to go to the circus.

One year, when it was time to arrange the annual family outing for LARC's staff and their families, we chose the annual appearance in Dallas of the Ringling Bros. & Barnum and Bailey Circus.

I got everyone great seats on the first several rows. I was sitting on the front row at the aisle and my mother was directly behind me. Just before the lights went out, she tapped me on the shoulder and asked, "What if the lion gets out? Lions and tigers get out."

I sighed. "Mother, the circus has been around for 103 years, and this has never happened." (It had, of course, but I didn't want my mother worrying, so I flat-out lied.) I turned back around to watch the circus.

At the beginning of the second act, the center ring had been prepared for the lions and tigers. I noticed a movement out of the corner of my eye, and—good grief! A lion was out. A trailer had pulled forward before its door shut, allowing a lion to come out of the trailer prematurely.

In the jungle, the mighty jungle, the lion sleeps tonight. Ours was wide awake, checking us out and looking a little bewildered.

Some of the crew ran past us, muttering, "The lion is loose."

None of this did much to calm the crowd. Or the lion. All were distressed. But before too long, the lion had been maneuvered into a cage, making both it and us much happier.

Finally, I faced the inevitable and looked back at my mother. Her eyes, peering over her glasses, said, "I told you so." She never said a thing. She didn't have to.

The next year, when the circus came to town, I asked my mother, "Would you like to go to the circus?"

"No," she said. But she did. In fact, she's attended almost every year. Where the circus is concerned, we're all children, and it really is the greatest show on earth.

CHAPTER THREE:

THE HOLE STORY

Shortly after President Richard Nixon opened trade with China, my company, LARC, was employed by the U.S. State Department to develop the first American-style amusement park in China. It was one of the first things on China's to-do list.

The Chinese traded $12 million worth of Chinese granite and marble to the United States for a $12 million amusement park.

They wanted this, for one thing, as a gesture of generosity to the people on the part of the Chinese government. Also, the Chinese people, once they grew their government-set quota of rice, were allowed to keep the money from selling the surplus. The government wanted to provide the people a way to keep this money in circulation.

So, we developed the Dragon Lake Park, a huge complex in Shantou that included a shopping mall

47

(basic, but on the mall principle), an eight-acre lake, a theme park, and the miniature golf course that is the topic of another of this book's stories. The Chinese wanted a very friendly park—nothing scary. The mall's prime anchor store was a forty-four-chair barber shop.

Within a $12 million budget, we were told we could come up with pretty much anything—except that the Chinese definitely wanted us to include a game they'd heard about from a missionary years earlier. This game was played with a stick and a ball.

We thought this might be softball, baseball, cricket, hockey, croquet—and we trotted out ideas for each of these to the Chinese, who shook their heads. That wasn't what they wanted. Finally, we figured out the

Michael and his Chinese colleagues celebrate the deal to build Dragon Lake Park.

48

game that had captured their imaginations: miniature golf.

So we went to work designing a course we thought would be quite wonderful—the eighteen wonders of the world. Yes, I know, there are only seven wonders of the world. But we came up with eighteen.

When the course was complete, we showed the Chinese officials. They didn't seem terribly impressed. Before long, I received an urgent call to go to Washington, D.C. to meet with officials at the Chinese embassy in hopes of averting an international incident. LARC had created some sort of dreadful problem that was going to have to be corrected immediately.

The problem turned out to be a cultural one. Acting according to the U.S. custom of saving the best for last and going all-out on the last hole of a miniature golf course, we had made the eighteenth hole the Great Wall of China.

The Chinese were not happy. Hole Number 18 was, to them, the least important hole. We had insulted the Great Wall. It should be the Number 1 Hole.

The problem was easily fixed. Our senior designer, Ron Shook, renumbered the holes in reverse order. The first became the last, and the last became first, and the Great Wall was the Number 1 Hole. The park, with its golf course, became a huge success.

THE EGG AND I

My personal physician is Dr. Kenneth Cooper, the well-known aerobics guru. Nothing would please Ken better than to get me out on the jogging track with my wife. Wendy runs up to five miles a day and is in wonderful shape.

Me, I'm afraid I might spill my martini.

More than likely, Ken would call me in for a cholesterol work-up if he'd seen what I ate one night at a Chinese banquet. In China, just about every time you eat, it's a banquet.

Sometimes you just want to grab a bite without a big production.

Anyway, there were eighteen people at our table, and somehow or other I'm the guy who got picked to start the festivities. First, I was presented with a huge silver pot. When they took off the lid, there was just one peanut inside. Then they offered me either a fork or a pair of chopsticks. I thought I'd give the chopsticks a go, in honor of being in their country.

After that, I got to try everything first. They gave me a thousand-year-old egg. It's not really a thousand years old—it just tastes that way. I was told that it's covered with hay and manure, wrapped in gauze, burned and buried for about four days. It's green like Jell-O and tastes . . . you don't want to know.

Let's put it this way: In China, eggs don't go over easy. I ate mine so fast—just to get it down—that my hosts thought I liked it. My reward was that they gave me . . . uh-huh, another thousand-year-old egg.

A SITE TO BEHOLD

Our Chinese amusement park, Dragon Lake Park, was to have a lake in the middle. So we had to build up the land around the sides of what would be the lake, raising thirty-four acres about forty inches and compacting the dirt.

We'd planned to send in some heavy equipment to do the job, but the Chinese said no, they'd raise the site themselves. All we had to do was come build the park on top when they finished.

Enter the Chinese army, armed with buckets. They moved buckets and baskets of sand to the site, pouring it out and stamping it down with their feet. They worked in a never-ending line, twenty-four hours a day.

Our LARC engineer determined that if our equipment had been used to do the job, and if it had worked every day—which it never does, because equipment breaks down—the company would have finished only eight days ahead of this group.

Chinese workers prepare the foundation for Dragon Lake Park.

Kind of makes me wonder if we should put the Chinese army in charge of road construction in Texas.

BIG WHEELS IN TOWN

The Chinese projected that about 2.5 million people might visit Dragon Lake Park, and they were quite pleased when 3.6 million actually attended that first year.

From our point of view, one of the most interesting aspects of the development was providing parking. We were used to doing parking lots—you figure 2.7 to 3.5 people per car, figure the acreage, the angle of the parking, etc., and come up with how many spaces you can create on an acre.

Chinese guests line up for a ride at Dragon Lake Park.

But in Shantou, the primary mode of transportation was the bicycle.

To show me the scope of the situation, my Chinese hosts took me to a soccer stadium. I was amazed to see a sea of identical black bicycles—not a one in a different color—all with identical bells and baskets, all made by the same manufacturer.

There were 108,000 people at that soccer game, and at least 100,000 of them had come on bicycles. There was an attendant for each of the forty bicycle racks, to make sure the bikes didn't get stolen.

What happened at the end of the game was an amazing thing to watch: All the fans came pouring out of the stadium, and each went to his or her own bicycle—which they seemed to find effortlessly, even though the bikes were all identical—and rode off into the night.

WHEEEEEEE!

This may shock you, but there are a lot of people in China. In fact, 3.6 out of every ten people on the planet are Chinese as I write this. Within six years, that figure is expected to be four out of ten.

There are more children under twelve in China studying English than the entire population of the United States.

And many of the people in China never stray far from home. More than 88 percent of all the people in China, I'm told, have never been 100 miles from where they were born—and that statistic takes into account the Chinese army of 4.6 million.

So I suppose it shouldn't have surprised me, when I awakened at 6:00 one morning in China, to see a four-block-long line of Chinese people waiting to get into the new, four-story, contemporary hotel in which I was staying.

It was a bleak, drizzly morning, and there they all patiently stood, waiting their turns.

Obviously, all these people weren't waiting to check in. The hotel had only twenty-eight rooms.

I dressed and hurried downstairs, where I discovered why the townspeople were lined up: The brand new hotel had what was at the time in China a modern marvel—an escalator.

Now, the Chinese have been ahead of the curve on many inventions. In this hotel, for example, we were issued keys that had to be inserted in a slot both to open the door and to turn the lights on in the room. When you left the room, you had to take the key, turning the lights off and saving electricity. This system is now in use in some U.S. hotels, but the Chinese put it into practice first.

But escalators were a western thing, and at this time, few Chinese had seen them.

So, on Saturdays—which this was—the hotel let the townspeople come in and ride the escalator from the ground floor to the mezzanine, from which they would journey, via escalator, back to the main floor.

Thus satisfied, many would go about their daily chores. But others would get back in line and take the ride again and again—just as they do in our amusement parks.

There was no sign saying "you have to be this tall to ride this ride."

NO *WHEEEEEEE!*

You've probably picked up on the fact that I spend a lot of my life being transported. Planes, trains, and automobiles are only the half of it.

On my second trip to China, where I visited a town named Shantou, I sat waiting for an airplane that was scheduled to come every two days. It would take me to Guangzhou. The plane never came, though, and about forty-five minutes after it was due, it was announced that the plane had crashed, with three passengers onboard along with a pilot, copilot, seventeen chickens, and a goat.

We waited, subdued by the bad news, for another two hours until we learned there would be no other plane for two or three days. The only way to Guangzhou would be by bus. I figured I'd take the bus.

After another hour and a half of waiting, the bus arrived and sixteen of us loaded in, sitting down on hard wooden benches. The trip to Guangzhou, we were informed, would take eleven hours. Eleven hours on a hard bench! I'll never complain about an overseas flight again, no matter how cramped.

All night long the bus bounced down bumpy roads, bruising my posterior with each bounce. We made two stops, during which the driver would tie a rope to the door with a knot on the end. Each of us took it, one by one, working our way to the end of the rope in the pitch dark to relieve ourselves, then, guided by the rope, coming back to the bus.

I arrived at Guangzhou at 6:00 A.M., battered and disgruntled.

I couldn't sit down the rest of the day.

SOMETHING TO SMILE ABOUT

Anytime I forget to pack my toothbrush, I go absolutely nuts. In the United States, our parents drill this tooth-brushing thing into us: We cannot go to sleep unless we've brushed our teeth.

It's not that way everywhere.

For a long time in many parts of China, the brushing of teeth was considered something to be done only on special occasions. In rural China, no one would consider actually brushing every day.

The Chinese government realized this was a problem and tried several approaches. At one point, toothbrushes were sent home with schoolchildren—who promptly shared them with everyone in the household. Clearly, this was not the answer.

But during the time that we were developing Dragon Lake Park, the government decided to put some real teeth into their hygiene campaign. It was ordered that every day, everyone *would* brush his or her teeth. All at the same time. That way, anybody who didn't do it would be noticed.

So, during the park's construction, at exactly 2:00 P.M. every day, a whistle would blow and everyone would stop what he or she was doing, whether it was pouring concrete, welding steel, painting, hammering, whatever. At that moment, each person would whip a toothbrush out of his back pocket and brush his teeth. Without toothpaste or water or anything. For five minutes, it was brush, brush, brush—up and down, up and down, up and down. Then back to work.

That was the government's new dental hygiene program, and it seemed to be working—at least for the manufacturers of toothbrushes. By now, perhaps, they're handing out toothpaste to the construction workers.

A CULTURE OF A DIFFERENT STRIPE

In the United States, we take a lot of things for granted. Like stripes on roads.

During the construction of the Dragon Lake Park in Shantou, China, I was driven to a meeting. There wasn't much traffic on the road, which was divided into bicycle lanes (two-thirds of the road) and vehicular lanes (one-third of the road). This road was in the process of being striped—by hand. I began to count the people I saw painting stripes on the road, and during the seven-mile drive, I counted 289 road paint-stripers.

Feeling sorry for the Chinese, when I arrived at the meeting I indicated that as a gift to the Chinese people we would, when we sent the amusement park rides over, include a road-striping machine.

I was trying to be nice, of course, but my Chinese hosts pleaded with me not to make this gesture. They explained that they did not want this technology. They wanted 289 people to have jobs. It was much more important to them to have 289 people painting the road all day than to have a road-striper do the job in forty-five minutes.

Of course, this made perfect sense. I shut up, went back to working on the park, and never mentioned road-striping machines again.

IT'S ALL IN THE WRISTBAND

You know about Murphy's Law of Lines, of course. Whatever line you pick at the grocery store will contain a woman using fifty coupons, and she'll have trouble locating her checkbook when it's time to pay. In the bank, your line will contain, if not a bank robber, at least a guy who doesn't have the proper identification to cash his check and will spend ten minutes pleading fruitlessly for an exception to the rules.

I'm no better at picking lines than anybody else. This story proves it:

I was going through customs in Hong Kong, and so were many, many people carrying everything from cans of oil to blankets to all types of items made in China. I despaired; this was going to take forever.

I spotted a man in a conservative gray suit. He looked like a boring IBM salesman. I placed myself right behind him, knowing he'd move through swiftly.

But I'd forgotten Murphy's Law of Lines. When his turn came, the customs agent told him to take off his coat and roll up his right sleeve. Reluctantly, he did— to reveal eleven Rolex watches, all the way up his arm. Clearly, this man was a smuggler.

What gave him away? A nervous tick? And why does someone become a professional watch smuggler, anyway? I'll never know.

I just know that I stood there, watching as the lines full of people with their oil cans, blankets, bamboo sticks, huge vases, and pots and pans moved on through customs, while I was stuck behind the guy in the gray suit.

A MEANINGFUL BOOKING

Some good deeds are rewarded. Richly—far beyond the simple acts they require.

In 1978-79, when President Nixon opened trade with China, he negotiated some cultural exchanges. One of the things they wanted from the U.S. was an amusement park, and that became a $12 million theme park called Dragon Lake Park. In exchange, the U.S. would receive $12 million in marble and granite from China.

LARC was retained to design and build the park. I met a translator who was with me for most of the first four trips that I made to China.

One night, on my second trip, while he was walking with me back to my hotel, he asked if he could step into the room and ask me a question. I said of course, and he came in.

He was extremely nervous. Carefully, he asked me if I could bring him some books in English from America, because he had already read every English book in the small library in this particular town and had a great interest in furthering his English reading and writing abilities. I agreed to do so.

On my third visit, before I left home, I went to the bookstore and purchased a Bible, a number of books on Washington, D.C. and the presidency, and one particular book he'd asked me for about "a lady with a big dress." I figured he meant *Gone With the Wind*. I also figured that one would occupy him for quite some time; it was as thick as one of those big skirts. I also took some books about Texas.

As I packed for the trip, I realized that getting these

59

books into China might be difficult, so I wrapped several of my shirts around them and buried them deep in my suitcase. Fortunately, the bags weren't inspected—remember, this was back in the '70s—and I passed right through.

My translator picked me up at the airport. Not a word was said. I checked into my hotel, and we attended our meetings.

That evening, he was looking at me questioningly but had prepared to leave. I asked him if he could come by my room. When he stepped inside and I began to pull out all these books, huge tears came into his eyes. He was so appreciative. He said he had heard about the Bible but had never seen or read one. He had heard about the women with big skirts but had never read about them.

He loved these books, and over the years I brought him more. I'm not sure who got the most out of this exchange—him or me. But I know he read them all. In fact, during the twelve years I knew him, I think he read *Gone With the Wind* three or four times.

WonderLand Park, Dubai.

Guests take a train ride at Dubai's WonderLand.

A wild ride at WonderLand in Dubai.

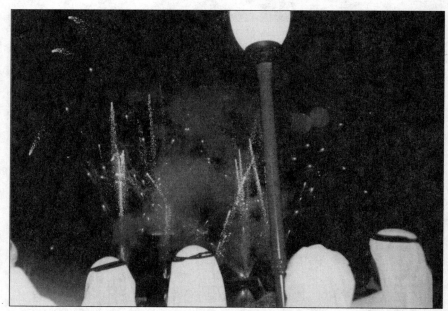

Over the heads of its Dubai guests, WonderLand Park shoots opening night fireworks.

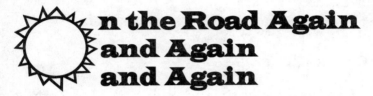

CHAPTER FOUR

On the Road Again and Again and Again

THE NIGHT THE CEILING FELL

Chattanooga's Rock City, a longtime client of ours, was doing great business. But the Chattanooga Visitor and Convention Bureau had approached us about enhancing the area's tourism with another project, the Tennessee Aquarium.

The tourism officials had put me up in a hotel that had recently been restored. I pulled the covers up over my head and went to sleep.

At about 4:15, I was awakened when something very heavy pounced on me. Sure that I was being assaulted, I scrambled to untangle myself from the covers, knocking over a lamp and wrestling in the dark with the unknown 115-pound assailant for several minutes before I realized that it wasn't moving.

My attacker turned out to be the ceiling. The hotel's

restoration had included new plaster on the ceiling. In the room above me, the bathtub had overflowed, wetting the new plaster, which eventually broke away and landed on me.

I was uninjured because I was so thoroughly encased in the covers.

One should never underestimate the true value of burrowing.

ROAD RAGE

I spend a lot of time in New York City, both as a producer of musicals and as a creator of amusement parks. I'm there between thirty and thirty-five times a year. I even lived there in 1963 and 1964 during the development of the Texas Pavilion at the New York World's Fair.

Spending a lot of time in New York inevitably means spending a lot of time in taxis. Usually, I am transported from place to place without incident.

But not always.

One of those not-always trips took place on a Friday afternoon. I was on my way to the airport, heading into the Lincoln Tunnel in one of those old Dodge taxis that had the little straps on each side, kind of like a street car. I never was quite sure why those straps were there. This was the day I would find out.

As we crawled slowly through the tunnel, which was its usual jam-packed self, we felt a jolt. A lady (I'll be nice and call her a lady) in a brand-new Cadillac Seville—it still had the sticker on the window—had rammed my taxi in the rear.

After being jolted, we inched forward with the rest of the traffic.

The lady rammed us again. And again.

After the third time, the taxi driver told me to take one of those little straps in my left hand and one in my right hand. I did.

He let the car in front of us get some distance ahead, then suddenly sped forward and threw the car into reverse, crashing into the lady in the Seville.

Then he did it again. And again.

When we got out of the tunnel, the police pulled everybody over for a little discussion of driving etiquette. Turned out the lady in the Seville was upset because—according to her—the taxi driver had cut in front of her before we entered the tunnel.

Guess she showed us: Her brand new car's front lights were hanging out by the wires and her grill was virtually demolished. On the taxi, however, there was not a scratch. Even the dirt on the bumper hadn't moved.

WHO'S SLEEPING IN MY BED?

I was in Atlanta for the convention of the International Association of Amusement Parks and Attractions. The acronym is IAAPA, which I suppose is roughly what you're supposed to scream on a roller coaster.

I was planning to meet our research manager, Jerry Windholz, but he was arriving early to attend a cocktail party. I called him at 4:00 P.M. Dallas time and asked him where he was.

"I'm at the cocktail party," he said, "at the Hyatt Regency."

"What's our room number?"

"1414."

So, I flew in late that night—the next morning, actually; it was nearly 3:00 A.M. by the time I arrived at the hotel. I took a taxi to the Hyatt, where I asked the lone desk clerk for a key to room 1414. I carefully opened the door, trying not to wake Jerry, who I knew would be sleeping. Sure enough, a sleeping form was sawing logs in one of the room's two beds.

I quietly brought my baggage in, tiptoed into the bathroom, changed into my pajamas, turned out the light and crawled into the vacant bed. About five minutes later, I heard several coughs.

"Jerry," I asked, "are you OK?" Silence.

Suddenly a light came on and a highly alarmed face—one I'd never seen before—was staring into mine.

"What are you doing in my room?" he demanded.

"I'm with Jerry Windholz," I explained, though the explanation did not make the man happy. He did not know any Jerry Windholz. He knew only that 1414 was his room, I was in it, and he wanted me out. He called security. I was informed that Jerry Windholz was not registered at the Hyatt. Nor was Michael Jenkins. The legal resident of 1414 had by now worked up a Category 5 huff. He wailed that he was sure I was there to rob him. Or worse.

The thing is, thieves don't usually change into pajamas. The Hyatt security guard apparently snapped on this, because he didn't call the police. Instead, he let me gather my belongings and trudge downstairs in my shoes, pants, and pajama top to check into another room.

After way too little sleep, I went to the IAAPA breakfast, where I ran into none other than Jerry Windholz.

"When we spoke on the phone yesterday," I asked through bared teeth, "where did you say you were?"

"The Hyatt Regency."

"They had no room for you at the Hyatt, and they have never heard of you," I informed him.

"Of course not," he replied. "We aren't staying at the Hyatt; we're staying at the Marriott, in room 1414. The cocktail party was at the Hyatt; that's all. Hey, where were you last night?"

Perhaps this would have been another appropriate time to scream "IAAPA!"

For the rest of the weekend, Jerry and I worked out a deal. He stayed in his room at the Marriott, and I stayed in mine at the Hyatt. It worked out great.

MEET THE BOSS

I make a lot of speeches. It goes with the territory in the tourism business.

I made one in Atlanta at the Georgia Governor's Conference on Tourism. The topic was future trends in leisure time and the entertainment market. After my speech to a crowd of about 600, the woman who'd picked me up at the airport came up and asked if I'd like to meet the president.

Thinking the president of the Georgia Governor's Conference on Tourism was in the hotel, I happily

67

agreed. So she took me upstairs and put me in a room, where I waited for a few moments.

The door opened, and in popped the president. Of the United States. Jimmy Carter.

Mr. Carter said he'd been able to catch a bit of my speech through a one-way mirror into our conference room (keep that in mind any time you're at a conference). He found my talk interesting and decided he'd like to say hello.

He asked where I was from. Dallas, I said.

"Did you vote for me?" he asked. I'm no good at lying, so I had to 'fess up. I told him I thought he was a wonderful president, but, truthfully, I didn't vote for him.

He laughed and put his arm around me.

"That's OK," he said. "No one else in Texas did either."

A CASE OF THE WILLIES

I met Bill Clinton in 1978 in Hot Springs, Arkansas, where LARC had built a small amusement park. The park has since been refurbished and is still in operation.

That day we were dedicating the park. Mr. Clinton, then governor of Arkansas, was there to attend the opening.

The owner and president of the park, Bob Sykes, was giving a speech. Behind him on a small platform, standing very close, were Governor Clinton and a woman from the chamber of commerce, who was clutching a plaque she was about to bestow upon me and Mr. Sykes. I was standing up there, too.

I'd brought along to the ceremony my seven-year-old son, Angus. I'd just bought him a camera, and he had brought it with him. He was sitting on a bench behind us, facing the audience.

As Mr. Sykes made his remarks, suddenly the chamber of commerce woman, who was standing to my left, jumped a little, seeming to contract a little case of the heebie-jeebies. I wondered if a bee had landed in her hair or something. But she soon settled down.

When Mr. Sykes finished speaking, the woman presented her plaque, seeming nonplussed and vaguely irked while she was talking. Maybe the bee was still in her bonnet. I made a few brief comments, and the governor concluded the ceremony.

As we were leaving the platform, young Angus asked, "Did you see what the governor did?"

"What did he do?" I asked.

"He put his hand on that lady's bottom," my son replied, eyes wide.

"I'm sure he did not," I said. "You must be mistaken."

"He did so!" Angus said. "I have some pictures!"

I immediately wound that roll of film off the roll, and when we got home, I hid it in a safe place—so safe a place that I lost track of it for a while. Probably just as well. But we still have it and plan to keep it, for its historical value.

I DON'T DO WINDOWS

It was a dark and snowstormy night.

I'd flown into New York late on a Sunday night. I

69

like to travel at night so that I don't waste those precious daytime hours that can be better spent in delightful meetings.

So I got into a Yellow Cab and headed for Manhattan. Just as the driver crossed onto Riverside Drive, he hit a bunch of huge potholes, no doubt caused by the lousy weather. At the last big bump, the back window popped out of the taxi. It was resting on the trunk of the car. Knowing it wouldn't stay there long, I jumped up on the seat and reached back to grab it.

Clearly, I had to communicate this unusual situation to the driver, but that was difficult because of the big sheet of Plexiglas separating us, protecting the driver in the event that I turned out to be a deranged killer. A killer I was not, but I probably looked pretty deranged hanging out the back of a taxi with a window in my hand.

Finally, I was able to kick the Plexiglas and attract his attention. He turned around, surveyed the situation, and yelled: "Let it go!"

Okey-dokey. Not my taxi.

I released the window and watched it slide off the trunk and onto Riverside Drive at midnight in the snow, cracking into a million pieces.

For the rest of the cab ride, snow fell into the cab through the hole where the window was supposed to be. I accumulated a small drift on the shoulders of my overcoat.

By the time I arrived at the Park Lane Hotel, I was my own snowman. The doorman helped me with my luggage and quietly brushed the snow from my shoulders. Only in New York.

ROADSIDE ASSISTANCE

Sometimes, instead of taking a taxi, I rent a car.

A rental car tends to be reliable, but, like any car, it has four tires. And from time to time, tires run over stuff and go flat.

So it was that I found myself one afternoon—again, on my way to the airport—with a flat tire on my rental car.

Instructions that came with the car said that in the event of road trouble, the driver should pull to the side of the road and raise the hood of the car to signal trouble. Someone would be along soon.

I did that. But I was in a hurry to get to the airport, so I figured it might be a good idea to go ahead and start changing the tire.

I'd been working on the project—the rear passenger-side tire—for about five minutes and had just gotten the lug nuts loose when a pickup truck suddenly swerved off the road up ahead, stopped, and then backed up at great speed to within inches of my parked rental car.

Out jumped its driver, who hurried over to me with a look of great concern.

"Oh!" he exclaimed. "You're getting the tires. All I want is the battery."

And he started toward the front of the car to get it.

I headed him off, explaining that the car was a rental with a flat, which I was fixing. He got in his truck and drove away.

I had no doubt that, had the car been on the side of the road for twenty-four hours, it would have soon been up on blocks with the battery, engine, CD player,

71

air bags, and anything else even remotely marketable removed.

That's why parked cars in New York City sometimes have the windows down and a sign on the dashboard that says it all: "Radio already stolen."

WE ALL DESERVE A BREAK TODAY

I've had a lot of fun working on various projects—many of them in Las Vegas—with an oilman named Johnny Mitchell, who was raised in Galveston and later moved to Houston.

One day we were driving to the airport in Dallas to fly to Houston. He asked me to pull into a McDonald's.

I told him the airport was only minutes away, and within an hour we'd be in Houston and could go get any type food we wanted. He still wanted to pull into McDonald's. So we did. Before he got out of the car, he asked me how many seats were on our plane. I said probably ninety.

Would they all be filled at that time of day? Probably not, I said.

To my surprise—and the utter shock of the kid who took his order—Johnny asked for sixty Quarter Pounder burgers. The kid didn't quite believe he was for real until Johnny paid up front for the burgers.

Johnny packed the burgers into shopping bags with handles and took them on the plane, where he passed them out to everyone on board. He had enough for all, with four burgers left over.

He felt obligated to do this, he explained, because darn it, he wanted a Quarter Pounder. But he didn't want to eat in front of the other passengers unless they were eating, too.

PHONEY BUSINESS

Johnny Mitchell had this habit. Every time he'd pass a pay phone, he'd reach into the coin slot. Finally, I asked him about it.

He explained that he grew up poor. He used to shine shoes and do other odd jobs to make money. He also learned that a lot of people left refunded coins in pay phones, not realizing they were there. So anytime he passed a phone, he made it a practice to reach in and see what was there.

It was a habit he couldn't break. He said he often picked up about a dollar a day that way.

AFTERNOON DELIGHT

Believe it or not, there are many times that I stay in a hotel and nothing the least bit strange happens.

But when you stay in hotels often enough, you're just going to run into some weird stuff from time to time. Here's another of those times:

Johnny Mitchell had invited me to Houston to go over some business matters and wanted me to stay in a Ramada Inn in which he was an investor. He dropped me off and said he'd be back in a couple of hours to take me to dinner. I checked in, got my key, and went up to my assigned room.

I unlocked it. There were two double beds in the

room, and I couldn't help but notice that one was occupied by a man and woman in the throes of passion. The man didn't even notice I was there. The woman looked over at me, and I announced: "Don't mind me. I'll just sleep on the other bed."

The man, totally unclad, jumped up, ran to the door, and slammed it in my face, barely missing my fingers, which were still on the door handle.

Hmm. OK, then. I went back downstairs and suggested that I be given another room. No, the clerk insisted, Mr. Mitchell wanted me to have that specific room because it was recently refurbished and one of their best rooms.

"But," I informed the clerk, "it's occupied."

"Impossible," he said.

"Go look," I said.

He did. The man and woman were still there. Turns out they were employees of the hotel. They'd noticed the room had been taken off the books for the day— probably because Johnny Mitchell had reserved it for me—and decided it would be a perfect place to consummate their relationship.

MUST BE THE FAN BELT

When you're an Arkansas traveler, you need to know the rules of the road. The rules are: You're in Arkansas. You love all things Arkansas. Don't forget that.

A friend and I were driving in Arkansas one day when a policeman pulled us over near Fayetteville. We pulled out our licenses. He took a quick look and then told us to slow down; he'd let us off with a warning this time.

He began to walk away, but stopped. Something about those driver's licenses . . .

"Where did you say you were from?" he asked. We hadn't said, but we assumed he'd seen our licenses.

"Texas," we said.

"Are you on your way to see the University of Texas and the University of Arkansas play basketball in Fayetteville?" he asked.

No, we told him, that was not our mission.

He informed us that the game was over, that the University of Texas had won, and that the result was entirely unfair.

And he pulled out his little book and wrote us a $135 speeding ticket.

 **tar Tales**

THE BREATHTAKING MISS CHANNING

It doesn't get much more fun than Carol Channing in *Hello Dolly*. And that was one of the first productions I presented to Dallas.

Miss Channing was very gracious and every bit as nice as that big smile of hers indicates.

She asked—not demanded, but asked—if I would consider letting her have three things during the run of her contract in Dallas.

I asked: What might those three things be?

First, she said, she'd like a washer and dryer separate from those used by the rest of the cast. I said that would be fine.

Second, she'd like a couch—a short couch, not a long one—so she could lie down during intermission and hang her feet over the side.

I agreed that would also be an appropriate request,

76

Carol Channing signs a book for her friend Michael.

though I said I'd be happy to get her a full-length couch so she could stretch out.

No, she said. She wanted her feet to hang over. Her third request, she said, was a small tank of oxygen. I was taken aback.

"Can you tell me why?" I asked.

She said it was really quite simple: She likes to wash her undergarments separate from everybody else's stuff; she likes to hang her feet over a couch at intermission; and during intermission, she likes to take oxygen to get her through the second act. Those three things, she assured me, were all it took to make her happy.

So we did just that.

On opening night, she came out of intermission into the second act blazing with energy. She did a fabulous job.

Backstage after the show, I thanked her for the remarkable performance.

"I can understand why you needed the washer and dryer and the short couch," I said, "but I probably need that oxygen more than you."

The reason being: Miss Channing's performance had left me truly breathless.

A DILLY NAMED DILLER

In the entertainment business, we deal with a lot of really difficult people. And that's putting it mildly. Many stars are known for making impossible demands, sometimes to the point where it seems they're trying to sabotage the shows they're in.

Instead of talking about those people right now, I'd like to talk about Phyllis Diller.

I've never seen anyone in show business work harder than Phyllis.

When she came to Dallas Summer Musicals, she was seventy-eight years old, and she seemed to have boundless energy.

We'd contracted her for the show *Cinderella*. No, she

wasn't Cinderella. She played the wicked stepmother—a role she delighted in. And she was wonderful.

She'd go out after the performance and have dinner until well past midnight, then we'd take her back to her hotel.

At 5:00 the next morning, she'd be on the phone wanting to know if we needed her to do a radio interview or television appearance to promote ticket sales. Heck, you have to beg most stars to do interviews. To get them to a morning show, you practically have to kidnap them.

Not Phyllis. She was always front and center, working harder than anyone else to make the show a success. She may have played the wicked stepmother in the show, but trust me: She was our fairy godmother.

A SHINING STAR

It was a coup to sign Tony Curtis to star in our recent musical version of *Some Like It Hot*.

Of course, we wanted to milk the publicity potential for all it was worth.

Tony played the part of Osgood, an eccentric millionaire, originally played by Joe E. Brown in the hilarious film, ranked as one of the funniest of all time. When I asked Tony to come to Dallas to do advance publicity, he agreed and chose the Easter weekend to come with his wife, Jill.

As it happened there was a large Turtle Creek program that weekend, in which the park was blocked off. For starters, there was a concert and a pooch parade.

I told Tony I'd like him to make a brief appearance,

Tony Curtis turns cowboy-for-a-day at Easter in the Park celebrating the Turtle Creek Association. He was in Dallas to appear in the stage production of Some Like It Hot.

but I think he misunderstood. He said he didn't want to appear in the middle of some metal Quonset hut with a dirt floor while barking dogs ran loose all around him. It sounded like Tony was afraid he'd step in something.

I explained to him that this wasn't a dog show at all, just a fun pet parade.

Tony looked dubious and said he'd stay for just ten minutes.

As we drove to the parade starting point with Tony in the front seat of a Lincoln Town Car, he seemed quite uncomfortable and out of place. At one point we were stopped in traffic and the car was totally surrounded by barking and yapping dogs.

I was nervous, but Tony looked absolutely miserable. "Do I really have to do this?" he said.

"I really need you to do this," I answered firmly.

"OK, but for no more than FIVE minutes," he vowed.

Since I'd made a promise that Tony Curtis would appear, I knew I'd have to take that five-minute appearance and run with it.

I got out quickly, went to the stage, and made my introduction before Tony was tempted to bolt and run.

And wouldn't you know it? Tony Curtis had a ball up there. He became so delighted at seeing the dogs decked out in all their wacky and resplendent regalia, he was cracking himself up. The man actually stayed on the platform for an hour and a half.

He'd worn his Texas hat, which endeared him to everyone, and he was happy to chat with fans and pose for pictures. He was the hit of the pooch parade.

DRAW YOUR OWN CONCLUSIONS

Our problem, that same Easter evening, was to find a nice restaurant that was open for dinner. Lots of places are open for Easter Sunday lunch, but we needed a nice evening meal for Tony Curtis and his wife, Jill.

Wendy had seen the maitre d' at the Mansion on Turtle Creek that afternoon to secure a reservation and told him that Tony had drawn on the menu the day before at the Crescent Club. Would that be a problem at the Mansion?

The maitre d' indicated that would be fine. The menus would not be left on the table, so there really wouldn't be anything to draw on. But he did stress that under no circumstances—under no circumstances—(he said it twice) could Mr. Tony Curtis draw on any of the new, linen tablecloths that had just arrived at the restaurant.

That evening we had quite a gathering at the Mansion, including our other two producers, along with Tony and Jill. For Easter, Wendy had given small gifts to the women, crystal eggs from Tiffany's filled with jelly beans.

And I had bought Tiffany pens for the gents.

Dumb move, Jenkins.

Tony liked his pen so much he began to clear away the dishes and draw on the new, linen tablecloth. Wendy was horrified at what was happening and looked like she'd seen a ghost, but she just kept smiling.

Tony was getting into his artwork so ardently that he even used the condensation from the water glass to smear onto the tablecloth for shadowing purposes. I must tell you the artwork was looking very, very good. Everyone was having a great time except Wendy, who knew what dire consequences would occur.

At the end of the meal, the maitre d' approached our table and Wendy whispered, "I guess you'll have to put that tablecloth on our bill."

"Put it on the bill?" the man scoffed. "After he signs it, I'm going to take it home and frame it."

I reached under the table for Wendy's hand, felt her wrist, and noticed she had a pulse once again.

Tony's rendering was a lovely work of art, really, a bouquet of spring flowers done in a sort of Matisse, impressionist style. His medium is linen tablecloth with a Tiffany pen. Must be a new art form.

SPAMMED

One of the great things about the Music Hall is that it is on the grounds of Fair Park, and during the annual fall State Fair, the performers get to enjoy the fair and all it has to offer.

One of the perils of the Music Hall is that it is on the grounds of Fair Park, and during the annual fall State Fair, performers wander off and get way too involved in the fair and all it has to offer.

Rick Hilsabeck, who has probably performed the title role in *The Phantom of the Opera* more than anyone else, happened to be performing in that show at the Music Hall during the fair one year, and he learned that the fair had scheduled a Spam cookoff.

Rick, it turns out, loves Spam. Yes, that strange,

pasty meat that lives in a little can opened with a key. Rick loves it. And he wanted nothing more than to be a part of that State Fair event. Sure enough, they signed him up as a judge.

I warned he'd have to be back and in his Phantom makeup by 12:30 P.M. for the 2:00 P.M. show. He agreed and trotted off to the Spam contest.

I next heard from him at 1:10. The contest was running a little behind, he said. He had tasted only forty-three of the sixty-three different preparations of Spam. I had no idea there were that many possibilities. I'd figured, actually, that there was only one: Take the little key, open the Spam and, if you must, eat it.

But no. Rick informed me there was fried Spam, blackened Spam, roasted Spam, marinated Spam—an infinite number of ways to prepare the stuff. He pleaded for more time to enjoy this culinary experience.

Absolutely not! I reminded him he was already challenging the makeup artists, who usually took an hour and fifteen minutes to complete his Phantom makeup. He begged. This was not pretty.

I called a backstage assistant and told him to take an electric cart and go get Rick. Twenty minutes later, Rick arrived, and as he was getting into makeup he became—imagine!—extremely ill. The Phantom was looking a little green, even under all that white makeup.

Rick's understudy went on that afternoon. (Here's a secret about understudies: They're almost always as good as the headliner, and sometimes they're even better.)

Actors can be fined for shenanigans like this, so Rick begged me not to mention it to company management. And I didn't. But never again will I let a performer loose in Fair Park on Spam-eating day. Never.

TUNING UP

From time to time, visitors backstage at the Music Hall might notice that we have red ribbons tied to all the ceiling sprinkler heads.

There is a reason for this. His name is Tommy Tune.

Tommy Tune, you see, is six and a half feet tall. If we didn't mark our sprinkler heads with red ribbons, he'd be constantly banging into them with his head. He might be seriously wounded. Or he might set off the fire alarm. We weren't sure. Since nobody had ever gone head-to-head with the sprinkler system before, we just didn't know what the effects of breaking off a sprinkler might be.

So every time Tommy comes to town, we break out the red ribbons and tie them on all the sprinkler heads.

Now, if we can just make sure his $6 million-insured feet don't trip over anything.

STARRING MR. GOODWRENCH

Dallas Summer Musicals' staff prides itself on service. We'll even fix a guest's flat, if called upon.

Sometimes our service policy extends beyond our guests' wildest dreams.

During a production of *The Music Man*, Barry Williams of *The Brady Bunch* fame was our professor

Harold Hill. He knew his way around the stage, but getting home was another matter. He seemed to have a talent for getting lost while driving back to his hotel.

So I asked him to call me every night when he got back to the hotel, so that I'd know he was OK. This he did, without fail. One night, though, he was very late calling. I asked where he'd been.

He said he'd helped some folks fix a flat tire in the Music Hall lot; they were parked next to his car. I thought that was very nice of Mr. Williams, but mostly I was just glad he'd made it to the hotel.

The next morning I received a call from a woman who wanted to thank me, because a member of our staff—true to our reputation—had helped her husband fix a flat tire on their car. Our customer service program, she said, was excellent. The man who'd helped them was very courteous and helpful.

I asked her to describe this nice man. Of course, it was Barry Williams.

Informed of this, the woman nearly dropped the phone.

"That was Barry Williams, the star, that fixed our flat!" I heard her scream to her husband. She asked if she could come back to the Music Hall and have Barry autograph the tire. He was pleased to do so, with a big white marker. One can only wonder what became of the tire, but this couple will always know they can trust their car to a man who is a star.

CASTING A SPELL

A show I remember with particular warmth is the

performance of *The King and I* in the late '90s in which Hayley Mills starred as the governess. My wife Wendy's parents came to see the show, and I took them backstage to meet Miss Mills, who was charming.

That afternoon, as I do with every cast, I thanked the cast of *The King and I* for being in Dallas and gave them a pep talk and a small gift. Because it was Sunday and they had a matinee performance, we gave them lunch to eat between performances. Very few theatres do this, but it takes the pressure off the cast to go find food and return to the theatre in time for the next performance. It helps us as well as them.

Michael and Wendy Jenkins with their pal, Mickey.

As my in-laws and I were later chatting with her, Hayley Mills said rather hesitantly, "Michael . . . no, you might not even consider this a compliment."

"Go ahead," I said. I've heard pretty much everything.

"Well," she said, "this afternoon when you were speaking to all of us, it reminded me of when Mr. Disney would come out and talk with his casts."

A compliment? To me, there could be no higher compliment. I have always been the world's largest Walt Disney fan, having amassed a collection of Disney ceramics, cels, and other rare memorabilia.

Wendy let her know quickly that she could not have bestowed higher praise on me. Hayley Mills has an invitation to come back to Dallas Summer Musicals any time.

YOU GONNA EAT THAT?

Sharing is overrated. It's a good thing, but it can be overdone.

When *Dame Edna* came to Dallas, the famous Barry Humphries from Australia came off the airplane.

We were told that Barry unfortunately had suffered a severe dental problem. He had broken his bridge.

At 6:30 on a Monday evening, it's extremely difficult to find a dentist, but we did find one, who repaired the bridge but suggested that Mr. Humphries eat lightly, so as not to dislodge it. Soup or mashed potatoes, the dentist suggested, would be most appropriate. The dentist suggested Al Biernat's, because it has great whipped potatoes. Although I rarely make my dinner plans based on my dentist's recommendations, I did this time, and with excellent results.

Al Biernat's has great food. Mr. Humphries ordered a bowl of mashed potatoes. I ordered the petite filet. Although small, it was a delicious and tender steak. Mr. Humphries could not help but notice the delight with which I was carving it.

He asked if he might have just a small piece of my filet.

I carved off a piece, and he ate it—successfully, because it was very soft and didn't require much chewing. He asked for another. Then another. I spent the rest of the evening cutting up my filet into small pieces and placing them on Barry's plate. Next time I take a dental patient to dinner, I'll bring along the dentist to glare at him.

THINKING BIG

Texas is all about being big, and the Music Hall at Fair Park is no exception. The place is cavernous.

So when Barry Humphries arrived for *Dame Edna*, he was a bit intimidated. He'd never played in so huge a theatre. The Music Hall was two and a half times the size of the Broadway stage he was accustomed to.

He was so nervous that we decided to take action. We raised the orchestra pit so he could play as close to the audience as possible.

It worked. His performance was magnificent, and since that day he's gone on to play other large theatres, without a hint of nerves.

THE GOSPEL TRUTH

The stage world is known for a lot of things, but devout practice of religion isn't one.

So it surprised some people when actress Jodi Benson, who was the female lead in *South Pacific* and also the voice of the Little Mermaid in the Disney film, became the first to lead a Bible study backstage on Sundays for the cast.

Did her fellow cast members give her grief? Not at all. There were plenty of takers for her Bible study class.

Michael and Roy Disney at Six Flags Over Texas.

A GENTLEMAN AND AN ACTOR

I have to admit it. Dallas Summer Musicals fans constantly amaze and confound me. Some of them just HAVE to get backstage to meet their favorite star. Oh, *ple-e-e-e-eze*.

Of course, it's my job to hear and judge these pleaded cases on an individual basis and certainly with a grain of salt. In my business, you really have to protect the performers and respect their privacy at all times.

When Tony Curtis played Osgood in the Dallas performance of *Some Like It Hot*, I was approached by a woman in the audience prior to the show. She asked if I'd give an envelope to Mr. Curtis. She said it concerned a very, very important matter.

There was something so earnest and intense in the woman's demeanor. I agreed to take the letter backstage with no promises that it would be read or commented upon.

I went on about my business, but I was aware of where the woman was sitting. At intermission, Tony Curtis asked me to come into his dressing room. He wanted to know if I could find the woman who had written the letter.

I said, "Yes, certainly . . . is there a problem?"

Then Tony silently opened the envelope and handed me the letter. It told of the woman's father, a man who had gone off to World War II with his wife pregnant back on the home front. The man had been on the same Navy ship with Tony Curtis but was killed in action before he could see his newborn daughter.

There was a picture in the envelope of the young sailor. Now his daughter wanted to know if Tony Curtis remembered her father. Did the wan, young figure in the picture look familiar at all?

Standing there with me, Tony looked at the photo for a long while, then asked me if he could see the woman after the performance.

I arranged for her to meet the stage manager after the show and be taken backstage. As it was a Sunday matinee, I left for nearby WRR Radio on the fairgrounds to do my weekly show.

When I arrived back at the theatre forty-five minutes after the performance, I was going through the stage door as the woman was leaving. She was wiping tears from her eyes, but there was a joyous expression on her face.

She thanked me profusely for helping her meet Tony Curtis.

When I saw him in his dressing room a few minutes later, he appeared pensive for a moment.

He looked up and said, "You know, I'm not sure I really knew her father, but I told her I seemed to remember him. It meant a lot to her. I think I may have met him. I do seem to remember talking to a guy who was excited that his baby daughter had been born, but he hadn't seen her yet."

There wasn't much to add as Tony and I stood there in a quiet moment. Finally, he said, "I felt like I needed to comfort her . . . to help bring closure to her."

That's all that was said, but I left with a renewed admiration and great respect for Tony Curtis.

Ann-Margret hugs her buddy.

Rich Little and Michael.

Michael with Salah Hassanein (formerly president of Warner Bros. International Theatres).

Michael and Wendy Jenkins and Deborah Norville.

94

CHAPTER SIX

Taking Nigeria for a Few Rides

MIGHTY FISHY SOUP

You've heard the old joke about the guy in a restaurant who complains, "Waiter, what's this fly doing in my soup?"

And the waiter says, "Looks like the backstroke."

If you ask me, this customer ought to quit whining. There are worse things that can pop up in a man's soup.

On this particular night I was dining at the Nigerian Federal Palace with the commissioner, mayor, and chief council person for the area where our theme park was about to be built. A man from the American Embassy was there, too. I was hoping I could bluff my way through Nigerian protocol. I was OK until the soup arrived—cool soup, at that.

As I lowered my spoon into the bowl, I thought I saw some shimmering movement. Yes, there was definitely something moving around in there.

The movement turned out to be several angel fish, and they weren't there by accident. I was told the fish were there to keep the herbs stirred up. You know how dull food can get when herbs just lie there.

Remember that Indiana Jones movie when Indy's girlfriend spotted eyeballs bobbing around in her soup? She reacted with a piercing scream—an entirely appropriate response.

The guy from the American Embassy told me I'd have to eat those fish or it would be an affront to our host. I told him in a friendly but firm manner that I wasn't about to. That's when I noticed everybody was looking at me . . . waiting for me to begin. I just kept smiling and nodding.

It occurred to me I might bluff my way through by eating just the broth, so I tilted the bowl halfway on its side and trapped two squiggling, little fish against the side of the wooden bowl.

That's when the embassy guy nudged me under the table and whispered harshly in my ear: "I'm telling you that you are going to eat those fish!" Nobody else was going to eat, he explained, until I did.

My smile was starting to crack like a WPA sidewalk.

I'm happy to report I did not endanger U.S. and Nigerian relations on this formal occasion. I came through—and once I ate that soup, I could do no wrong in the eyes of the Nigerians.

But I'll never forget how those two fish felt as they wriggled across my tongue.

Trust me, you don't want to know how two live angel fish taste as they swim south down your gullet. All I can say for sure is this: it certainly isn't the same as sushi.

After Michael returned from a trip to Nigeria during which he was forced to eat live fish, his staff bought him one to just feed and watch.

BIG WHEEL KEEPS ON TURNIN'

We built an amusement park near Lagos, Nigeria, for the government—in fact, it was the first amusement park in Nigeria. It had a big Ferris wheel. We were prepared to go one morning and teach the local workers how to operate the wheel.

When we arrived at the site at 7:30 A.M., we found the workers perched on seats on the Ferris wheel. They had climbed up the 5½-story ride and onto the wheel, where they were sitting and rocking in the chairs. They had never seen such a ride and had no idea it revolved.

We blew a whistle and got them to climb down from

the ride so that we could explain. Once the wheel began to turn, they were overwhelmed. They began to smile, clap, and laugh. They had never seen anything like it.

With its lights on in the evening, the Ferris wheel proved enormously popular. However, most of the Nigerians preferred to stay on the ground and just look at it. They were afraid of heights.

A JOB FOR DAD

The simple fact was that most Nigerians had never experienced an amusement park. Rides weren't just something unfamiliar; they were frightening. Imagine seeing a carousel for the first time: horses going up and down, with the ride turning and generating loud music. It was exciting, but scary.

When the park opened, we found that families would come and simply stand and look at the rides. The father would take the first ride, alone. We learned this was to prove in front of his family that he wasn't afraid of anything. Once he emerged from the ride un-injured, his family could ride.

This worked out fine, except on the kiddie rides. These rides aren't designed for full-sized people. Many fathers simply could not fit on them. Those who did put a tremendous strain on the equipment. Neverthe-less, many adult Nigerians loved the children's rides.

In fact, they loved them so much that when the ride was over, they didn't want to get off. They just stayed in their seats, intending to keep riding and riding. Thus, we were obliged to teach Nigerians about the concept of getting off the ride and getting back in line. It's not the most popular process in an amusement park, but it's essential.

TUNNEL VISION

In the amusement park in Nigeria, we built an Antique Car Ride, where the driver could sit in the car with his family and navigate a make-believe turnpike, moving the car eighteen inches in either direction but on a course stabilized and directed by a guide rail.

On opening day, we noticed that when the car entered a tunnel, the Nigerians would jump out and run around the tunnel, waiting to jump back in the cars when they emerged from the tunnel.

This, of course, would not do. It wasn't safe. We had to shut the ride down.

What we learned was that there was a rumor among the Nigerians that the Americans were waiting in the "cave" to club them in the dark. They were afraid to go in the tunnel.

So we cut skylights into the ceiling. That solved the problem, and the guests stayed in their cars through the entire ride. Nobody's been clubbed yet.

NAME DROPPING

On a very long and very boring flight from New York to Lagos, Nigeria, I decided to read my passport. (It was either that or the seat belt instruction card.)

I noticed a blank that asked for the name of a close

*Apapa Park in Lagos, Nigeria
(the first amusement park in Africa).*

friend or relative to be contacted in the event of an emergency. So I filled in a name: Bee Lyn.

When I arrived at the airport, we landed, disembarked, and were given a ride to the airport on a little wagon like the ones used for hayrides, only there wasn't any hay. And the ride wasn't nearly as much fun without hay, I must add.

But we did get to the main terminal. When I got to the head of the passport inspection line, the passport inspector took a look at mine and frowned.

"How long," he asked, "have you known Bee Lyn?"

"About eighteen years," I said.

"Do you like Bee Lyn?"

"Yes," I said, for at the time I liked Bee Lyn at least well enough to want Bee Lyn to be contacted in the event something happened to me on an airplane.

"Come with me," he said, and took me to an interrogation room where, for the next hour, I was asked all sorts of questions about my relationship with Bee Lyn. I could not imagine why the Nigerians were so curious about my friend, but I answered their questions.

Finally, the man from the American Embassy who was supposed to pick me up and had been waiting for me to come out of the terminal realized something was up. He came in and started asking questions.

He soon found me and was able to extricate me from the Bee Lyn interrogation.

Once we were clear of the airport, he explained: Bee Lyn was the name of the mafia chieftain of Lagos. Everybody thought I was big friends with this guy— whom I'd never met.

Needless to say, my current passport makes no mention of Bee Lyn. If anything happens to me on an airplane, Bee Lyn will have to hear it second-hand. Next time I write down the name of a contact, I will Bee Careful.

I'M FOREVER BLOWING BUBBLES

When they tell you "Don't drink the water," believe them.

On this particular trip to Nigeria—to the towns of Lagos, Apapa, and Ikoyi—there was an outbreak of cholera in the region. This was nothing to mess with.

Our instructions were clear. No water could be consumed under any circumstances. In fact, this was before bottled water, as we know it, was commonly used. We had to employ alternative liquids.

So, there was a warm, not chilled, imported English beer that we used to brush our teeth. The more you brushed, the more it foamed and gushed. After brushing my teeth, I found myself wiping my mouth every ten minutes.

By the time a car picked me up to take me to a meeting, I thought I had at last stemmed the flow. When I arrived at the state building, I was taken to a meeting room on the first floor. Many African children crept up to the windows to look in and see the American man sitting in the room.

When I turned around and smiled at the children, they let out a yell and ran away. Hey, I like kids, and normally I'm pretty good with them. Whatever happened to the old Jenkins charm?

During a break in the meeting someone discreetly explained the problem. It seems I was still frothing.

Apparently, when I had opened my mouth as I turned toward the window, a big bubble floated out of my mouth. The kids had every right to fear a stranger who happened to be foaming at the mouth.

ACCEPTED EVERYWHERE

Sometimes this job leaves me feeling like George of the Jungle. Watch out for that tree!

I had to travel seven miles of rutted road in a Jeep to get to a dense jungle where no vehicle could go, just so I could hike three more miles to meet a tribal chieftain.

Sometimes my job boils down to shaking hands with the right people. We wanted, and needed, the chief's approval for the building of the first amusement park in Lagos. Local participation and approval is important to us.

As we finally entered this remote African village, I was amazed to see an American Express sign nailed to the side of a primitive building.

While I talked with the chieftain, I couldn't help staring at that sign all through our conversation. Finally, I interrupted our talk to ask about that sign.

The chief had his own question. Where could he get more of those American Express signs? They were just the ticket for patching up holes right after the rainy season.

Who wants to live in a leaky hut?

The American Express folks were providing more of a service than they knew, although I'm sure they weren't getting their usual percentage.

American Express: "Don't leave home without it."

IT TAKES A THIEF

I was rolling down a street in Africa in an official American Embassy car when we came upon a truck. I noticed the brand name on the back of the truck: ANGUS.

I was amused. I'd never heard of that brand of truck, and Angus is my son's name. I thought I'd take a picture of the truck to give my son.

So I lowered the window, leaned out, and pointed my camera. As I was snapping the picture, four Nigerians jumped from the back of the truck and began screaming and flailing about.

The American Embassy driver stepped on the brakes immediately, pulled a quick U-turn, and headed back in the direction from which we had come. He was very unhappy with me and told me never, ever to take a photograph without consulting him.

Seems there's an old belief among some Africans that when their picture is taken, the photo captures their spirit. I was truly sorry about this.

I was also worried, because the dispirited Nigerians were pursuing us on foot at high speed down the highway. We finally outran them.

Someday, I would like to return to Nigeria, hunt those guys down, and relinquish their spirits to the rightful owners. Think maybe they'll let me keep the negatives?

CHAPTER SEVEN:

Up, Up and Awry

THE LADY AND THE LAVATORY

Even high in the sky, nature calls. On this particular day, it was summoning a lady sitting across from me near the front of the plane. She'd never flown before, and the flight attendant had to show her where the restroom was.

When she went in, I noticed the light didn't come on indicating the lavatory was occupied. The reason was that she hadn't closed and latched the door completely. She was holding on to the door, but keeping it open a crack, maybe to let more light in from the airplane, maybe because she didn't know how to latch it—who knows?

A few minutes after she entered the restroom, the flight engineer emerged from the cockpit. Apparently, nature was calling him, too.

Seeing that the door sign said "vacant" and was

slightly ajar, he pulled on the door. It didn't move. He grabbed it with both hands and yanked it. He yanked it open all right—and also yanked the lady out into the plane's aisles, on her knees with her pants down.

Suitably mortified, the lady dived back into the restroom and slammed the door shut. This time she got it latched—with the engineer's tie caught in it.

He knocked on the door and asked her to please release the tie. No way was she going to open the door.

Finally, the flight attendant took a knife from the galley and sawed the guy's tie off. Hey, he was the flight engineer; he couldn't spend the whole journey standing by the lavatory. Back to the cockpit he went, his stub of a tie sticking out like a bow tie.

Over the drone of the plane's engines, we heard uproarious laughter coming from the cockpit.

The pilot soon emerged and tried to console the lady and get her to go back to her seat for landing. Nope. She was in the restroom, and in the restroom she would stay.

This marked the first and only time I've ever seen a plane land with someone in the lavatory.

When the plane landed, I dawdled around to see what would happen. I was the last one off the plane, but when I left, the lady was still in the restroom. I'm not sure how—or if—they ever got her to come out.

CROCODILE HUNTER

A man with a lady's hatbox. You don't see many of those.

So when a man carrying a hatbox boarded the

Miami-to-Dallas flight I was on, taking a seat across the aisle and one row forward from me, I was intrigued.

Handling the box with great care, he placed it in the overhead compartment and buckled his seat for take-off.

After we'd been in the air for a while and had finished dinner, the man got up, reached into the overhead compartment, and retrieved the hatbox. He began to unbuckle its strap. I watched with great interest: Was he about to put on a hat at 30,000 feet?

But when the guy got the box open, his eyes widened in amazement and alarm. He immediately hit the button to call the flight attendant, and when she arrived, he showed her the box and whispered in her ear. Her eyes nearly leaped out of her head, and she raced for the cockpit.

Seconds later, the captain came on the public address system: "Ah . . . folks: It seems a crocodile is loose on the airplane."

A crocodile! Loose on the airplane! Almost every passenger, envisioning a six-foot, man-eating reptile, began to scream, flail, and engage in mass seat belt unbuckling. Twice the pilot assured us there was no cause for alarm. No cause for alarm—what a croc! There's a crocodile on the airplane! You can tell us there's no cause for alarm if the plane's flying sideways and you can't find the runway, and that's fine, but when there's a crocodile on board, there is cause for alarm!

I'm not a screaming kind of guy, but a good case of the screams is always contagious. I screamed along with everyone else, without having any idea why. Where is Steve Irwin when we need him?

The croc in question, of course, had emerged from the hatbox the man across the aisle had been carrying. He had purchased the reptile in Florida and was taking it home to Dallas. (Clearly, this was before the current security measures went into effect; these days, the crocodile's teeth alone would disqualify him as carry-on baggage.)

Later in the flight, the escaped crocodile was found sleeping peacefully on a blanket in an overhead compartment near the one from which he escaped. He was about a foot long.

The cold-blooded passenger disembarked with the rest of us in Dallas without so much as a "see ya later, alligator." By then, we'd all quit screaming. But hatboxes on airplanes still make me nervous.

A WING AND A PRAYER

Anytime you fly to Las Vegas, you know the flight is going to be a party with wings. Everybody's in a good mood, drinking, getting ready for a big time in Vegas.

The flight home is another matter.

I flew from Las Vegas to Chicago one day with a stop in Albuquerque along the way. The flight departed at 7:00 A.M., and you can imagine the mood. Most of the passengers had been up all night gambling and partying, and it was a tired and motley crew that boarded the plane.

The flight from Vegas to Albuquerque got rough, to say the least. Albuquerque is always a windy area, but this time, the plane was bucking like a rank bull on the rodeo circuit. Those who'd been drinking all night were reacting as you'd expect: groaning and turning khaki-faced.

In the middle of all this, a woman in first-class, who appeared to be in her eighties, unbuckled her seat belt, got down in the middle of the aisle, knelt, and began to pray. Loudly. This immediately attracted the attention of other passengers, who thought maybe she had some information they didn't have. So they got nervous.

Now, every time the plane hit a severe bump or downdraft, the people on the plane would yell.

And the lady would pray.

The flight attendants tried to get her to sit back down. She would not. The captain came out and appealed to her to take her seat. She would have none of it. Warding off the captain with her hands, she continued to pray.

And every time there was a violent motion in the plane, everyone else would scream. Yes—me, too. And I knew better. As one of the nation's most frequent fliers, I'd endured endless turbulence—some far worse than this—and knew we weren't all going to die. But again, screaming is contagious. You scream, I scream, we all scream.

I would tell myself I had to get hold of myself and settle down. I would. Then we'd hit another bump and off we'd all go, screaming like we were on a roller coaster.

And the old woman just kept on praying.

Finally, we landed in Albuquerque. About a third of the passengers, including the praying lady, got off and declined to continue the flight to Chicago—which, once we left Albuquerque, was one of the smoothest rides I've ever had.

PILLOW TALK

The thing about people sitting next to you on airplanes is that a lot of times they want to be your new best friend. Sometimes one actually will become a new best friend. Then there are other times when the relationship ... well, here's what happened:

I was on my way from Dallas to Japan in the first-class compartment of a brand new American Airlines 767, sitting next to a Japanese woman who never, in her entire life, had been on an airplane. She'd taken a boat to the United States, then a bus to Tennessee to attend a wedding. But some emergency had made it necessary to take a plane home.

I tried to help her out, adjusting her air vent, turning on her reading light when she needed it, etc. She needed a lot of help and explanations, with everything from lunch to the in-flight movie, but happily she could speak English, so I was able to answer her questions.

At one point the flight attendant pulled the shades down on the airplane to let us all get some sleep. On this nice new plane, the first-class chairs were designed to recline into beds. The Japanese woman had no idea what to do with hers. I helped convert her chair into a bed and pulled a blanket over her, pretty much tucking her in.

I did the same for myself, and we slept for much of the journey to Japan.

When we landed in Tokyo, of course, all the Americans were in one customs line and the Japanese travelers were in another parallel line—within shouting distance. Unfortunately.

The lady suddenly began to yell, "Mr. Jenkins! Mr.

111

Jenkins! It was very nice to sleep with you!" This she yelled again and again, while around me eyebrows did somersaults and mouths dropped open.

"Nice to sleep with you, Mr. Jenkins!" She continued through the entire immigration process.

I have since adopted a new blanket policy: From now on, I'll let my fellow passengers tuck themselves in for the night.

TALK ABOUT ATMOSPHERE

Some pilots don't say a lot when they're in the air. Others wear your ears out, talking about what you're flying over, what's on the left side of the plane, what's on the right side of the plane. (And speaking of that, how come the panoramic views of Lake Powell are always on the opposite side of the plane? I can't see Lake Diddly.)

Then there was the pilot on one plane I flew from Chicago to Los Angeles. Shortly after takeoff, he came on the public address system to make one announcement: Within an hour or two, we'd be flying over the Grand Canyon. When we were over it, he said, we'd know it.

OK. We all proceeded to read, sleep, and such.

Almost two hours into the flight, the captain came on the P.A. again. He made no announcement. He simply began to play his harmonica—the "Grand Canyon Suite." And he sure played the Grand Canyon sweet.

We looked out our windows and realized that we were, indeed, over the Grand Canyon. The whole plane applauded.

UP WITH GOOD GUYS; DOWN WITH MEANIES

I've always believed that the customer is always right. I practice that philosophy, even when the customer is a royal pain in the posterior.

Customer service is the very heart of any business that involves the public. And I can't illustrate the point any better than with the following airplane episodes.

In the first incident, I was sitting in the very first row of the coach section on a plane out of New York. Nice guy that I am, I won't name the airline. But the plane itself was a big orange one known to its employees as "Fat Albert."

A man came onto the plane. I recognized him as the airline's chairman. He walked to the third seat on the aisle in first-class and demanded that the passenger seated there get up and move to another seat; that was his seat. The passenger refused to get up.

The flight attendant didn't know what to do, and the head steward, too, was intimidated. The pilot came out and asked the man to move. The man would not.

Finally, the gate agent came on the plane and offered the man some unbelievable number of tickets if he would just move to the coach section. This time, the man agreed to move. But the whole situation caused a lot of huffing and harrumphing in first-class.

Later in the flight, I noticed the poor flight attendant in the galley between first-class and coach. The airline chairman threw a roll at her, demanding a hot roll. His, he said, was cold.

At that point, the man sitting in front of the chairman stood up, turned around, and told him if he didn't shut up, he would shut him up. The entire first-class cabin applauded.

The chairman got up and spent the rest of the flight riding in the cockpit jump seat.

Many years later, I was on a night flight from Dallas to New York, this time on American Airlines. I was sitting in first-class, in an aisle seat.

At the very last minute, before the door closed, I saw a man hop on the plane and crawl across my seat to sit in the window seat next to me. I recognized him: Bob Crandall, at that time chairman of American Airlines.

He was carrying a stack of papers more than ten inches high, which he kept on his lap and worked on, feverishly, during the flight.

When the meal was served, he noticed the man across the aisle from me hadn't eaten his steak. He asked me to get the guy's attention.

He asked: Was something wrong with the steak? Can we take it back and fix it? Would you like something else?

The passenger said no, the steak was fine; he'd just decided he wasn't hungry.

Mr. Crandall excused himself and walked up and down the aisles of the plane, talking with passengers, asking them how the airline could better serve them. He had a genuine concern for the passengers that impressed me very much.

Soon after I took that first flight, the airline with the big orange plane was out of business. Forever. American Airlines, of course, continues to be one of the world's dominant airlines, with an excellent track record of customer service that continues beyond Bob Crandall's tenure.

The philosophy, which I've adopted over the years: Customer service isn't everything—it's the only thing.

JUST PLANE LUCK

I shouldn't have laughed when I read about the American traveler who thought he was flying to Oakland but wound up in Auckland.

True story. The man was stuck in New Zealand waiting for the airline to fly him home for free. He claimed the mix-up was the airline's responsibility, not his own.

Sadly, it was nobody's fault but my own when I took the red-eye to Atlanta one night and changed planes to get to Charlotte for a morning speech. The planes for Charlotte and Charleston were loading from the same door but on separate ramps. Guess which ramp I shuffled down by mistake?

I didn't realize my error until the pilot announced we were landing in *Charleston*. I scrambled out of my seat, ran through the airport, and got the very last car as the rent-a-car place was closing. They were actually flipping off the lights as I rushed up to the counter.

I drove all night from Charleston up to Charlotte, arriving at 6:15 A.M., just in time to shower and rush off to give my early-morning speech.

I've had people nod off during my speeches, but this time I was the one doing the yawning.

Afterwards, I drove to the Charlotte airport to turn in the rental car. (There was an added top fee, of course.)

Totally exhausted, I was walking onto the plane

headed for Dallas with a stop in Atlanta. (In the South, they say if you die and go to heaven, you still have to go through Atlanta.)

As I slumped into my seat, the man sitting in the window seat turned with a big grin, stuck out his hand, and boomed, "JOHN SMITH! (or whatever his name was). I'm in insurance!"

I must have cringed. Here, all I wanted to do was curl up in the fetal position and go to sleep, but now I was trapped by a glad-handing salesman, sitting right next to me.

Clearly, he was preparing to talk my ear off all the way to Dallas if I didn't do something. So when he asked, I told him I was in the carnival business, figuring that might discourage him.

"Terrific!" he shot back. "My cousin just inherited a cave near Georgetown, Texas, and we don't know what the heck to do with it. Maybe it can be turned into some sort of attraction."

Well, of course, the man yammered unceasingly all the way back to Dallas. But you know what? Somewhere along the line I started listening to him.

And believe it or not, six months later we hammered out an agreement that turned into a nice project for LARC. The cave he was talking about became Inner Space Caverns, a well-known tourist attraction in Central Texas.

As Edward Albee once said, "Sometimes it's necessary to go a long distance out of the way in order to come back a short distance correctly."

116

CHAPTER EIGHT:

SAND TRAP

You remember the lament of the Ancient Mariner: "Water, water everywhere, and nary a drop to drink."

Well, if you can substitute sand for water, that's pretty much the way we felt while trying to construct a water park at Messilla Beach in Kuwait. All the way to the Arabian Gulf, as far as we could see, there was nothing but sand—for all the good it did us.

Oh, it was great stuff for making foundations and pouring concrete, all right. The problem is that these grains of sand, blowing for centuries, become very sharp-edged and abrasive. No matter how smoothly polished the final finishes were done, the surfaces of the swimming pools remained highly abrasive.

You can't have your guests all scratched up merely by getting into and out of the pool. Just rubbing your hand along the edge of the pool revealed how coarse and rough the surface was.

So we are the fellows who brought coals to New-castle. After much research we realized the local sand simply wouldn't do. We had to import red, smooth sand from India. I'm not at all sure we could sell refrigerators to Eskimos, but I'll be remembered in Kuwait as the man who hauled in sixty-eight tons of sand to a desert.

THAT FIRST STEP'S A DOOZY

My first trip to the United Arab Emirates was so weird, it's a wonder I ever came back. But to tell you the truth, I'm always a little curious to see what strange thing is going to happen to me next.

Maybe that's what keeps me coming back.

Anyway, LARC was invited to Abu Dhabi regarding a future entertainment project, and getting there was half the fun.

Did I say fun? First I flew to London and changed planes to take Gulf Air to Abu Dhabi. While I was wait-ing in the London airport, I bought a *Time* magazine. Thumbing through it, I was surprised to see a piece re-garding the minister of transportation in Abu Dhabi taking a $10 million kickback from a major aircraft manufacturer. It was a big, headlined story of an inter-national scandal. I put the magazine in my briefcase to refer to later.

Thirty minutes prior to our flight to Abu Dhabi, those of us on the plane were asked to move to the very rear of the aircraft. Two security guards with military weapons came on the plane and draped a sheet across the interior to prevent us from seeing what was tran-spiring in the front.

I mean, I'm used to the curtain between first-class and coach being pulled, but this time I really wanted to know what was going on up there. A doctor came on board, and we assumed that someone very important in first-class was getting special attention. We flew all the way behind that veil. And once we landed, we had to wait half an hour for the sheet to be removed. An ambulance came and picked up the special passenger, then the rest of us were allowed to deplane.

I never learned who the special secret passenger was. Heck, Howard Hughes was already dead.

Inside the airport, I was told to come to my hotel immediately, only to find out upon arrival that it would be two or three days before I would be allowed to talk to the reigning dignitary.

The hotel manager assured me I would have no trouble. "We're sending up twenty pounds of pistachio nuts and a case of Compari," he boasted.

You know I hate to complain, but after three days of Compari and pistachio nuts, I was ready for something else. Beer and pretzels would have been a nice change.

Finally, the big day approached and the minister of tourism came to advise me on protocol and local custom. I was told that bowing lower than your host is a sign of respect, and flashing the bottoms of your shoes or feet means you wish your host a quick and untimely death. I decided to stand with my feet planted firmly on the ground.

So, off we went to the palace to meet the sheik and maybe even do some business. I was introduced with a flourish by the minister of tourism, and then the sheik moved several steps toward me, stopped suddenly, and demanded to see some form of identification.

Identification? Did he think I was some guy *pretending* to be Michael Jenkins?

As I opened my briefcase to locate my passport, the sheik spotted the *Time* magazine.

"Oh, I see you've been reading about my minister of transportation," I was told.

He had me there. "Yes, your highness," I replied.

Then he startled me with his next remark: "My minister is very, very stupid. I can't believe how stupid he is."

I just stood there, not knowing what to say.

"He's so stupid," the sheik continued, ". . . because he could have gotten a lot more than $10 million."

I thought I would burst out laughing, but somehow I managed to keep a poker face.

And I'm glad I did. The sheik never cracked a smile as he continued the diatribe against his minister. He was seriously, seriously angry.

Men and boys frolic in the pool at Kuwait's Aqua Park.

Aqua Park introduced Kuwait to the concept of the Old West.

KEEP OFF THE GRASS

After presenting my credentials in the new city of Abu Dhabi, I began hearing of how the town was built from scratch. It just popped up. Already there were 60,000 people living in it. In the very center of town there was a circle, sort of like a round-about in London, and it took up perhaps an acre of space in the middle of the highway.

Now they were in the process of laying grass and watering it.

I noticed there were poles strung up with wire to guide people as they walked along the new area. Scores of people were walking back and forth along the grass with their sandals off and big smiles on their faces. I was told they had never seen grass before, and they loved the experience.

Well, who among us doesn't enjoy the feel of grass between our toes?

When I was leaving town on that very trip, there was a thirty-minute delay at the airport. A new cargo carrier had come in to unload huge pallets of grass—no doubt to replace the grass that had been trodden down to bare nubs by the delighted townspeople.

Is there really any such thing as progress? First, you get grass, and before long you have to put up a "Keep Off the Grass" sign.

IT'S NOT EASY BEING GREEN

People go to Carnival in Rio de Janeiro for all sorts of reasons. Mine was all business. Really, it was. No, honest.

I was there to look at a new form of transportation—a monorail-like people-mover that ran on top of the tracks. It was much lighter than a bus, much more efficient, and it had an air compression system making it impossible for two people-movers to crash into each other. It was truly remarkable, but because it was conceived in Brazil, many folks in the United States, unfortunately, weren't taking it seriously.

But I was in Rio to check it out, and so was John Broome, who was then chairman and chief operating officer of Alton Towers, the largest amusement park complex in the United Kingdom. We just happened to be meeting during Carnival.

We were walking from our hotel to a restaurant when we saw a Brazilian woman walking toward us in an extremely low-cut green sequined dress. She had green glitter glued to her face. Remember: It's Carnival.

She stopped in the street, put her arms around John Broome, and gave him a big ol' smooch. Being a proper Brit, he was right embarrassed. I was just relieved it hadn't happened to me.

When we got to the restaurant, I pointed out gleefully to John that he had green glitter on his face. He was so horrified he went back to the hotel to wash it off.

When I saw him later that evening at the hotel, he still had green glitter in his ear. I informed him. He showered again.

The next morning, as we were heading out to Port Alegre to check out the people-mover, I couldn't help remarking that there was still green glitter on John. The same was true on the way back from Port Alegre. The man was beyond chagrined.

When I got back to Dallas, every time I wrote John I'd have my longtime secretary, Wanda Beth, sprinkle a little green glitter in the envelope. Eventually he begged me to stop, and I did. But I doubt if I'll ever be able to look at him again without seeing green.

HAVING AN ICE DAY

One of the rewards of my work in developing amusement parks all over the world is getting to see each country's unique cultural and artistic offerings.

My hosts are always eager to show them off, and I'm equally delighted to see them.

But for the life of me, I couldn't figure out why I was trekking up a huge mountain in the dead of winter one day in Japan, in the Tottori Prefecture, where I had gone to look for a site for an aquarium.

On an expedition I'd been assured would be pleasurable, I was taken to Mount Daisen, the highest peak in the district. Up it we trudged, and I didn't know why. My hosts insisted I would be pleasantly surprised.

I was. About 1,500 feet up the mountain was a plateau. On that flat space had been constructed huge, awe-inspiring ice formations, some two and three stories high, glistening under lights. The Japanese had built ice houses, using ice blocks moistened and frozen together, with rooms you could walk into. Castles and dragons and sea serpents also towered on this plateau, some thirty feet high. They were spectacular.

Definitely worth the trudge.

OF WAX, LARGE CATS,
AND VERY BAD BEHAVIOR

You know you have a strange life when you can tell a story that involves a leopard, and the leopard isn't the scariest part of the story. That's the kind of life I have.

A number of years ago, LARC decided to build a wax museum featuring the presidents of the United States. The presidents weren't going to just stand there, though, as presidential replicas normally do. John Tyler would be playing marbles with his children,

124

as he had reportedly been doing at the moment he learned he'd been elected president. Harold Taft would be in the bathtub, because he'd had the first one installed in the White House—and had gotten stuck in it. Harry Truman would be playing the piano. That sort of thing.

I flew to Vancouver, British Columbia, to meet with Doug Cundy, Canada's foremost wax figure maker. It was the middle of winter, incredibly cold. I checked into the St. George Hotel, and Mr. Cundy picked me up for dinner at 7:30 P.M. I couldn't help but notice all the windows of his station wagon were iced up; that's how cold it was.

His wife was sitting shotgun, so I crawled into the back seat. Before long, I felt something huge, with a tongue that seemed to be about a foot long, licking me. Yes, licking.

I turned around to see that there was a leopard in the back of the station wagon. I nearly jumped out of the car, but my host assured me the big cat was just a pet and probably—probably—wouldn't bite me if I didn't act afraid.

Too late. I wasn't acting. I was afraid. But I tried to act unafraid. I looked straight ahead and held my breath every time the leopard licked my neck, which it did copiously.

I was highly relieved when we got to the restaurant. When Mr. Cundy asked if I'd like some wine, I was only too happy to take him up on it.

"Let me order," he said, "but don't be surprised at anything I do."

He ordered a very expensive bottle of wine, about $150, and the wine steward brought it, opened it, and poured some for Mr. Cundy—who promptly had a fit. He coughed, he choked, he spat, he made faces. His wife seemed bored by the whole thing.

The wine steward, alarmed, grabbed the bottle to whisk it away, but Mr. Cundy recovered from his coughing fit enough to stop him.

"What are you going to do with that wine?" he asked.

"I suppose I'll pour it down the drain," said the wine steward, whereupon Mr. Cundy offered to buy the wine for half price.

This, not riding with a leopard, was the low point of my night. I wanted to crawl under the table and, as we were leaving, I tried to make myself small.

The usually playful Michael Jenkins gets serious during a wine-tasting event.

Back in the car, I almost welcomed, by comparison, the company of the leopard, who continued to lick me all the way back to the hotel.

By the way, Mr. Cundy did wind up making our wax figures. We built the museum, and it was later sold to a gentleman who moved it to Galveston, Texas, where it caught on fire and all its residents melted.

BARKING UP THE RIGHT TREE

Trammell Crow, one of Dallas' best known and loved developers, is a good friend of mine. He once called me right before Christmas to see if I'd be available between January 11 and 16. I was.

"Meet me in Cancun between 12:00 and 2:00 in the airport," he said. "I'll be there to meet you." Then he hung up. I hadn't even caught what he'd said, but my secretary, Wanda Beth, had heard him on the speaker phone and told me.

I figured I'd better call his secretary to confirm before trotting off to Mexico, so I gave Elsa, Mr. Crow's secretary, a call. She said Mr. Crow had just left for the Christmas holiday, but yes, he intended for me to meet him in Cancun—and bring a bathing suit, tennis shoes, slacks, and maybe a jacket for dinner.

So, I flew down to Cancun, and Trammell and his wife Margaret were there to meet me. We went straight to his yacht, the *Michaela Rose*—the most fabulous yacht I've ever been on. We cruised down to Belize and Guatemala.

One day during this idyllic vacation, Trammell turned to me and said, "What the world needs is more trees."

"Trees?"

"Trees. We need to plant a million trees a year in the United States," he said, waxing on about trees' ability to balance oxygen and carbon dioxide in the atmosphere. Mr. Crow can always talk knowledgeably about just about anything.

"When I get back," he said, finally, "I'm going to talk to George about this."

About five months after we got back to the United States, during a flight to New York, I opened *USA Today* and noticed a story: President George H. W. Bush had announced the planting of one million trees. Trammell Crow was to head the project.

Oh. *That* George.

Michael Jenkins with his two long-time assistants, Jenny Cagle (left) and Wanda Beth.

SEA HUNT

On the beautiful cruise to Guatemala with Margaret and Trammell Crow on their yacht, we were sitting out on the boat's deck one day when Mr. Crow announced that he believed the future of the world was underneath the water. We'd already explored all of Earth and the moon, he said. But we knew little of what lay beneath the sea.

"Do you scuba dive?" he asked me. No, I said; I'd snorkeled some in Tahiti. But I'd never been scuba diving.

"I'll teach you," he said. He took me inside, sat me down, and offered about an hour's lecture on the intricacies of scuba diving. Then he announced he was going to take a nap for an hour, and when he got up we'd go scuba diving.

He walked off, then turned in the doorway with these parting words: "The only hard thing about scuba diving is that you have to hold your hand over your mask when you fall off the back of the boat to keep water from getting in." Then he walked off to take a nap.

No doubt he slept well for the next hour. I was immobilized by terror. That was a huge yacht; it must be three stories from the back of the boat to the water. I had no desire to hurl myself backward off the back of that boat. No, I wasn't going to be able to do this. I just couldn't.

After about an hour, Trammell emerged from his nap, stretched, yawned, and announced it was time to go scuba diving.

"Trammell," I said. "I would do anything in the world for you, but I just don't think I can fall off the back of this boat."

"What are you talking about?" he asked.

I repeated his parting words about holding the mask on while falling off the back of the boat.

"Not *this* boat," he said. "We're going to lower a small rubber boat into the water. It's about eight inches from the water." Oh.

So off the back of the little boat we went, down about forty-five feet into a perfectly peaceful dive, during which my host was attentive to my dials and actions. It was a great introduction—and in no way a scary one—to the wonders of the undersea world.

A MUTED MUTINY

Carrying around a lot of baggage is not fun. Definitely not fun. So when I buy something overseas, I like to ship it home. That way, I don't have to carry it, and when it arrives back at the house, it's almost like Christmas to open the package and get a surprise.

But on a particular thirty-day trip around much of the world, my traveling companion was of a different persuasion. She wanted to carry the world on her shoulders—or mine, or the hotel valet's. In New Zealand, I approved the purchase of an additional big red bag in which to carry some purchases. Turns out there was a bag within that bag, and another within that, and before long all three were filled.

Our last stop before we headed to Los Angeles was a brief stop in Tahiti. I didn't really want to go to Tahiti, but I was told it would be a quick overnight stop.

We arrived in Papeete and prepared to take a boat to the island of Moorea, where the film *South Pacific* was shot. By the time we arrived on that dock in Tahiti, my companion's bags had grown to sixteen. I had just a briefcase and hanging bag.

When the dockmate emerged, he inquired, "Where's the rest of this tour?"

While my companion trotted off to the restroom, I informed him it was only the two of us and suggested that most of our bags could be stowed overnight; we'd only need a few things.

"But," he said, "the boat doesn't come back for a week."

A week? Impossible. I had to go back to the United States immediately. This would not do, would not do.

But it would *have* to do, because that's the way things were. The boat wouldn't be back for a week, so we'd be in Tahiti for a week. I felt tricked. I *had* been tricked. So I sulked.

"I need a telephone," I said, planning to rearrange my carefully planned life.

More bad news: The telephone pole had blown down six weeks earlier and hadn't been repaired. That also meant no telexes. (This was long before the days of faxes, cell phones, and laptops.)

Steam was coming out of my ears.

The dockmate was calm.

"Have a banana," he suggested. "Have an orange. Relax. It's OK."

Off we went to a village where we were installed in a grass hut right by the ocean. I tried to sustain my huff as we snorkeled on a reef that held as many breathtakingly colorful fish as an aquarium.

The second night, I was awakened by my companion's discovery that there was a three-foot lizard on the ceiling. It was, of course, my job to deal with it.

I threw my shoe at it. I missed the lizard, but the shoe fell back down and hit me in the head. Hard. I needed stitches.

I was mad.

But somehow, staying mad in Tahiti was impossible.

After a couple of days, I found myself having a glass of wine at sunset on the beach, and I discovered I was actually enjoying myself. I forgot about all the emergencies in my little world back home, forgot about how many bags I was going to have to schlep through the airport, and I truly relaxed.

Did I mention that the women sunbathed nude on this Polynesian Island? Well, I should have, because they did.

It was the finest vacation I ever had.

AHOY, MATEY

During one of my early visits to Dubai in the United Arab Emirates, I learned as I was walking along the port that Dubai, at that time, was one of two ports in the world that allowed pirates.

Pirates, yes. Yo ho ho and a bottle of—never mind about the bottle; this is an Arab nation and they frown on that sort of thing.

It happened that while I was walking along the port, I was approached by an actual pirate. I knew by his outfit that he was a pirate. He'd obviously seen plenty of pirate movies. Ahoy, matey. *Arrrrrrgh!*

He even announced as he approached me that he was a pirate. And proud of it. He proclaimed that he and his pirate friends had just stolen 200 Honda motor scooters off Japanese ships. They liked to steal from the Japanese, he said, because the Japanese generally didn't fight back.

He and his pirate friends, he said, had 100 of these bikes they were willing to sell for $100 each. Would I be interested?

Truly, it did sound like a good deal. But then I realized that if I bought a bike from this pirate, he would probably just steal it back. So I passed.

To this day, every time I see a Honda scooter, I wonder if it might have been one I could have owned. Briefly.

WHALE OF A TALE

Call me Ishmael. Or don't.

But the fact is that back in the late '60s I found myself in search of a killer whale. Oh, I didn't have to hunt it down and harpoon it as in *Moby Dick*. Quite the opposite: I needed it alive and well. It was for a sea life park LARC was designing.

We made the complicated arrangements to snare one off Victoria Island, near Vancouver in British Columbia. There were spotters up and down the coast, and they'd spot whales migrating south and alert us.

Six weeks earlier, nets had been strung 100 fathoms deep in Peddler Bay from one shrimp boat to another 500 feet out, and then to a third another 300 feet out. Algae had grown on these, and the idea was that the whales would perceive them as a barrier—in fact, they could easily swim right through—and the boats could herd them toward the center of the bay.

Finally, whales migrated into the area—five of them, including an albino whale. The shrimp boats began to corral them. Excited, we flew to Victoria Island to greet the whales.

During the evening, though, someone cut the shrimp boat netting, allowing three of the whales to leave, including the albino whale. This albino whale was a rarity, and a national magazine had been on its way to photograph it. We did get a staff picture, but of course, the national magazine couldn't use that, worrying that it might have been doctored.

Still, we had two whales, one eighteen feet and one twenty-two feet. We soon became fond of them, feeding them mackerel and herring and scratching their bellies—they loved that. Killer whales? These guys were pussy cats. Pussy cats with ninety-six coned teeth that could easily rip you apart if they wanted to. But they didn't want to. They were very docile.

When their training began, they were fed butter fish as a reward. It was like giving steak to a dog; they were nuts for butter fish and would work to get it.

Finally, it was time to load them into a C5A airplane to be flown to Marineland on the Canadian side of Niagara Falls. This involved putting the huge mammals in a sling, from which they were lowered into a large crate of water. Another large crate of clean water had to be sent along with them. Why? Because, we learned, whales release fifty-five gallons of urine every twelve hours.

These beautiful mammals, whom we'd come to love, were babied all the way to the other side of Canada, rubbed constantly with cold cream and kept in clean water until they reached their destination. And they're a whale of a great attraction at Niagara Falls, Canada.

RENT-A-WHALE

One thing about whales: Any time a job involves one, the project's likely to wind up being all about the whale.

Our foray into Sicily started out to be all about tourists. LARC was commissioned by the Italian government agency SITAS to develop tourist projects in Italy, including one particular site in Sicily, in the town of Sciacca.

SITAS had built two lavish resort hotels on the coast, complete with spas, saunas, and mud baths. The town was lovely; the resorts were lovely. In situations like that, guests in Italy traditionally end their vacation by re-booking for the following year as they're checking out. But that wasn't happening at these resorts, and the government was puzzled.

After extensive research, they found that a vein of cold water runs through the Mediterranean—much as the jetstream runs through the air—and banks off the coast of Sicily, precisely at Sciacca. There, the water is extremely cold, approximately 38 degrees Fahrenheit. The guests could drive three miles in either direction and the water would be warmer; so that's what they were doing.

To get Sciacca's guests to come back again even though they couldn't swim in the sea, the SITAS agency decided it needed a water attraction. Something big. Killer whales are big. They decided on a killer whale

135

pool. LARC had a lot of experience with developing attractions around large sea mammals, so we went about
designing the whale pool, and we arranged to acquire a
killer whale that was caught off the coast of Iceland
near Keflavik. The whale was approximately 4½ meters
long, had no scars, and was being trained in Iceland.

As the construction of the pool was nearing comple-
tion, there was a lunch meeting with the government,
the mayor, and several business leaders. Meals are big
deals in Italy, of course, and as usual, this lunch
started late and lasted forever.

Toward the end of the lunch, a lot of yelling
erupted back and forth across the table (again, not unusual in Italy). I didn't grasp what was going on until
later: The town's mayor would not give approval for
the pool to be filled unless he received some monetary
benefit. The government would have none of it. For
three months, the project was hung up while the mayor
and the Italian government yelled and gestured at each
other.

At this point, the situation became all about the
whale. I kept getting calls from Iceland: We needed to
move the whale. Winter was setting in. Ice was beginning to form. Iceland is tough to get in and out of once
it's encased in ice for the winter.

So, here it was late November, our fabulous whale
pool in Sciacca lay empty, and our whale was sitting
around twiddling his fins in Iceland while ice crystals
formed around him. He would have to move, and soon.

Happily, a serendipitous solution arose. I got a call
from the owner of a park called Playcenter in Sao
Paulo, Brazil, that LARC had designed in the mid-'70s.
Playcenter had a dolphin show, but the owner said the

audience had grown tired of it. Might I have anything else I could send him to entertain guests in the area that the dolphins had been using?

Half seriously and half jokingly, I asked the owner if he'd like to rent a killer whale. Entirely seriously, he said yes.

Long story short, the whale was transported from Iceland and has remained in Brazil in good health. The whale pool continues to sit empty in Sciacca. And I can now add "whale rental agent" to my ever-growing job description.

THE SORCERER'S APPRENTICE

There's a little magician in all of us. We just have to know how to use it.

When LARC was in Kuala Lumpur, Malaysia, designing the new SamaWorld that was being built on top of the Genting-Highlands mountains, we were dealing with two brothers, Lim Tuck Fatt and Lim Tuck Sing.

The Lim brothers had a large conference room with twenty to twenty-five staff people, and every time I was in Malaysia, they wanted a presentation on what the park would look like. They knew; I'd told them before. But they wanted a presentation every time.

And at one point, the same question was always asked: Where was the parking?

Well, I'd told them time and time again about the parking. It was part of the master plan, and there was nothing unclear about it.

Still, the question from Lim Tuck Sing was always, "Can you explain the parking?"

After giving the presentation a number of times, it became obvious that we should not try to anticipate this question and answer it in advance, because even if we did, the query would pop up: "Can you explain the parking?"

Back in Dallas, as I prepared for a trip to Malaysia, I decided to make an impact this time with my explanation of the parking. I spoke to my friend Mark Wilson, a famous magician and teacher of many magicians, about how to add a little flash to my presentation.

He helped me rig up something: In my left pocket, there was a battery with a wire running inside my shirt to my right arm, down my right arm and out my sleeve, where I would hold some flash powder in my right hand. (Yes, you're right: I wouldn't be allowed on an airplane with this stuff today. But this was years ago; I had no trouble getting all this paraphernalia to Malaysia.)

It was time for the usual presentation to the Lim team. I launched into my long, laborious explanation, and as I eventually pointed to the exact place where the parking would be, a huge fireball came out of my hand, ignited by the battery. I acted as if nothing had happened and continued droning.

After the presentation, Lim Tuck Sing came up and stared at me. He looked at my hand, which was clean, with no burns or stains.

He never asked about the parking again.

SHEEPISH IN NEW ZEALAND

Nobody likes a guy who comes late to the theatre—not the folks he has to walk over to get to his seats, not the usher who has to maneuver him into place, and certainly not the performers.

So I was distressed to find myself late arriving for a performance of a Maiori dance in New Zealand. The Maioris discovered New Zealand, coming from the Hawaiian Islands. It's hard to imagine, considering how long it takes to fly to New Zealand, that these Maioris left the Hawaiian Islands in canoes and traveled for six months to get to New Zealand. (I was told that the priest who blessed the group as it left decided to stay home with the women while the men searched for a new world. Hmmmm.)

But back to the Maiori dance to which I'd been invited: I was late, and to my horror I learned that they had reserved a seat for me in the front row. Of course, the last thing I wanted to do was walk down to the front row and sit there, because it would be so distracting to everyone and so painfully obvious that I was LATE.

I was, however, encouraged to do so. Down I went, plopping down as unobtrusively as I could.

I looked up on-stage and noticed, with great mortification, that all the dancing Maioris were sticking their tongues out at me as they danced. Clearly, I thought, they were mad. I'd been late, and they were mad.

Later, of course, I learned that Maioris always stick their tongues out during their dances.

Oh.

I'LL HAVE THE GIRAFFE, RARE

About the time you think you've seen everything,

life sticks out a big foot in your path and sends you sprawling.

Some years ago, LARC was contracted to redo the zoo in Caracas, Venezuela, at the request of the wife of the president of that country. This was a gift for the children of the region, a slam-dunk project for our design team, which had just finished a similar job in Madras, India.

When I visited the project, I was startled to see federal troops arriving in late afternoon, just about sunset. The soldiers fanned out in orderly fashion to entirely surround the facility. Was there an insurrection among the higher primates? Bad gnus travel fast. I couldn't imagine what was going on.

A member of our design team had to explain that the evening shift had arrived. A nightly brigade of armed troops was sent there for a good reason—to protect the zoo animals from the local citizens. If there was no protection, I was told, some renegade locals would soon be climbing over the walls to kill and drag away the animals for food.

Hearing this, I stood there with my mouth open. Thank goodness, nothing jumped in.

CHAPTER NINE:

Tough Acts to Follow

PRODUCER-TURNED-FAN

I suppose everyone growing up has a hero, idol, mentor, or exemplar. Whatever you choose to call him, my man was David Merrick.

When I was in college studying theatrical management, Mr. Merrick was the foremost Broadway producer of his day, a respected lawyer and businessman, as well as impresario of the Great White Way. I read everything I could get my hands on about him. He was, indeed, *The Abominable Showman*, as one book about him was titled.

I always hoped I'd meet him one day even though he had a reputation for being a forbidding, even frosty character.

My chance came many years after college during the Broadway opening in 1996 of a successful revival of *The King and I*, starring Lou Diamond Phillips and

Donna Murphy. The Dallas Summer Musicals was an investor in the Dodger Theatrical production, and we completely recouped our investment.

Approximately 1,600 people attended the opening night cast party at the Marriott Marquis Hotel. After everyone settled in, the doors swung open dramatically and an immaculately dressed, solitary figure strode slowly into the room.

It was David Merrick, and was he ever dressed for the part—natty in his splendid topcoat, tuxedo, white gloves, top hat. The room fell silent as he was ushered to a reserved table where he sat by himself after deftly removing his hat, coat, and gloves.

I was standing with Miles Wilkin, who was chairman of Clear Channel Entertainment at the time, and who is now based in London.

"My God, that's David Merrick," I told him.

"I know," Miles replied.

I said I'd truly like to meet the man I'd read about for so many years. Miles said that's well and good, but nobody just walks up to David Merrick and starts a conversation. It simply wasn't done.

Miles was acting as though David Merrick were some sort of foreign potentate. I admit I didn't understand the protocol of the situation, but maybe I just chose to ignore it.

Later, as I walked by Mr. Merrick's table, I thought he looked a little lonely. Perhaps I was just imagining that, but I found myself walking over to introduce myself.

"Mr. Merrick, you don't know me, but I'm Michael Jenkins of the Dallas Summer Musicals. You've always been my hero, and I do believe I've read virtually everything ever written about you."

Mr. Merrick looked up a little dubiously and said in a barely audible voice, "Tell me one thing, just one thing you know about me."

He was testing me, of course, and I promised myself I wouldn't babble if given the opportunity to speak. So I mentioned the first thing that came into my head. It was the memory of a brilliant marketing move he pulled early in his career. His show *Subways Are for Sleeping* had not gone well. The reviews were uniformly pans. So Merrick had gone out and found seven people with the exact names of the New York critics. He invited them and their families to the show, sent out a limousine to fetch them, bought them dinner, and took their pictures. And after the show he got a favorable quote from each of them about the production. A few days later a full-page ad appeared in *The New York Times* with the names of the seven critics beneath pictures of Merrick's guests. The ad claimed seven of seven loved *Subways Are for Sleeping*. The right names, certainly, but not the right people.

I told Mr. Merrick I thought it was a brilliant move, one even P. T. Barnum might have cheered. He smiled and said, "Sit down, lad."

"That was a pretty good move, wasn't it?" he agreed. "I had to slip that ad into the newspaper on a Sunday evening when nobody noticed, or it wouldn't have run at all."

We chatted a few more moments and then, not wishing to intrude, I left him to his solitude.

Not long after that night, a matter of months, he passed away. I was so grateful I'd seized the opportunity to speak with David Merrick, however briefly. It was a moment I'll cherish the rest of my life.

UNCOMMON SENSE

When a troupe of Chinese acrobats appeared at the State Fair of Texas in 1986, it was a real coup for LARC. We were the first to form a partnership to bring the acrobats out of China and present them in the United States, and believe me, we had to jump through hoops, stand on our heads, and wriggle into all sorts of contortions to make it happen.

These guys were incredible acrobats. They'd been trained from the age of two, and they were as close to perfect as I'd seen. Any mistake would bring great shame on the acrobats, so they were under a lot of pressure.

Apparently, the intense acrobatic workouts limbered up their minds as well.

Our contract with the Chinese government regarding the acrobats specified that we had to do two things every Thursday: take them to the grocery store, where they invariably stocked up on rice, and take them to the post office so they could mail all the letters they'd written home.

I accompanied them to the post office the first time. They looked around as they walked in. Through the translator, they asked me: "Who are all these people whose pictures are up on the wall?"

"These are very bad people," I told the translator. "They have done bad things, and the United States is looking for them, trying to find them to punish them."

The acrobats looked at me quizzically and spoke briefly with the translator, who asked:

"Why didn't you just keep them when you took their pictures?"

They really had me there.

DOGGONE CRITIC!

One night at the Music Hall, during a production of *Grease* starring Sally Struthers as the teacher, an usher came rushing to my office beneath the Music Hall's auditorium.

"There's a dog upstairs," he said.

"I know," I sighed. "But the show will be over on Sunday night."

"No, I mean a real dog," he said. "There's a real dog in the balcony. And every time Miss Struthers sings, it howls."

I grabbed a couple more ushers, and we trekked up to the balcony to learn that the account was true: There was a dog, and he was howling every time Miss Struthers sang. We ran the dog down the stairs to the ground floor. Just as I opened the door to let him out, the door to the orchestra section of the auditorium opened and a man emerged on his way to the restroom.

Seizing the opportunity, the dog bolted through the door into the orchestra section, heading straight for the first row. When Miss Struthers began to sing, sure enough, the dog howled.

We chased him outside and thought that was the end of it.

But after the show, Miss Struthers met me backstage and asked where, oh where, had that little dog gone? She wanted that animal.

I suggested that might be a bad idea. We didn't know whose dog it was, whether it was infested with fleas or worse.

But fifteen minutes later, as the bus at the stage

door was leaving to take the actors back to their hotel, a security guard said Miss Struthers wanted to see me. There she was, standing in the doorway of the bus holding the dog in both arms. It had shown up at the stage door, and she, by golly, was taking it home.

Each Christmas I get a card from Miss Struthers with dog prints on it.

WHEN IT RAINS, I'M POOR

We brought in the mother of all rainmakers for our production of *Singin' in the Rain*.

The miracle machine is expensive and tricky. We even installed a heater so the raindrops hitting our actors would be warm instead of cold. What a glorious feeling: They're happy again.

Me, I'm a little nervous. With this water-making system there's always the chance something will malfunction. For instance, you have to prime the pump to make the rain come down. The machine is from New Jersey, has a capacity of using 500 gallons a minute, and it can sink Molly Brown or keep the *Titanic* afloat, if necessary.

The water is caught and recycled. It creates some puddles, then drains through the cobblestones.

We brought in an engineer, plus technicians, to supervise the showers. The device has safety switches that are supposed to shut down the system if the stagehands do not push the machine—it's a set, actually—into the proper position onstage.

But no system is foolproof. One night, the crew

forgot to fill the rain machine with water. So when the famous Gene Kelly scene came due, our actor wound up singing in the sunshine. Oddly, the audience didn't seem to mind. Nobody demanded a rain check.

TAKE A BOW

It's not always the stars who provide the warmest moments in the theatre business.

One Saturday afternoon our students from the Dallas Summer Musicals School of Musical Theatre were performing before the show. During intermission, in the lobby, a man I did not know walked up to me and asked if I were Michael Jenkins.

"Yes," I said. "I am." I'm asked that a lot, and I never know what's going to follow.

"Do you see that young girl on the far left on the second row?" he asked.

I said that I did.

"That's my daughter," he said. "I want to tell you something. My daughter was so shy and nervous that when she had to give a book report or hold up her hand or recite something at school, she would get sick and refuse to go to school. We decided to put her in this school, not knowing what would happen. She'll never be a star; she'll never be a great performer. But now she's the first one to raise her hand and stand up in class. It's helped her so much, and I want to thank you."

I've never had a more rewarding moment in the theatre.

BEHIND THE SCENES

Talent, of course, comes from everywhere—not just from families who can afford to send their children to acting school.

We heard about a young boy living in Southeast Dallas and wanted him to come to the audition for *South Pacific*, but he wasn't able to because he didn't have any transportation. So we sent a car to pick him up.

He came in and sang and was magnificent—perfect for the character of Emil, one of the children in *South Pacific*.

We took an interest in this young man and learned that his father had run off and left his mother, him, and two sisters in a home that had no indoor plumbing and had cardboard over the windows to keep in the cold air in the summer. Their circumstances were very difficult.

For an entire summer, the young man was able to tour with *South Pacific* from Dallas to Atlanta to Pasadena. While he was gone, his mother would spend the entire year taking in washing and ironing to support the family. Through a number of our staff people, we've been able to help his family out a bit. They now have indoor plumbing.

LISTEN TO YOUR MOTHER

My mother was always both my greatest supporter and my most severe critic. She usually attended a Thursday or Sunday matinee performance. She loved to sit in the back, not too close, and she didn't miss a thing. She was quite astute, and always let me know what she thought about each production on the way home.

148

I had a production of *Ragtime* that I thought was really good. (Actually, I think all of our productions are really good.) Mother saw it. While I was taking her home, she said not one word. This was driving me nuts. Finally, I couldn't stand it any longer.

"Mother," I asked, "what did you think of *Ragtime*?"

"It was OK," she said.

"Just OK?" I asked, disappointed.

"No," she said, "it was very good. But you have way too many people on the payroll, and you're going to lose your shirt."

I asked her what she meant by that. She noted that usually there were twenty-eight to thirty-four people in a cast, but in this production, with understudies and people who played two and three parts in the ensemble cast, there were forty-eight people.

"It's way too many," she said. "You're going to lose your shirt."

I said to her: "With all due respect, I know a little more about it, and I don't think you know what you're talking about."

Hmph. She didn't say any more, and I didn't say any more. But after I let her off at her condo, I immediately sped back to the Music Hall to look at the payroll records. Sure enough, there were forty-eight people in the production. As she predicted, we lost our shirts.

A BREATHTAKING PERFORMANCE

Those *Riverdance* performers are amazing, aren't they?

I never could get over the fact that they could tap twenty-eight taps per second. To tell the truth, I

149

thought this was impossible. But they actually video-taped it and ran it slowly back to prove that they did, indeed, hit twenty-eight taps per second.

Every show, they'd put on a dazzling performance, working and tapping like mad—only to step off-stage afterward, lie down on their backs behind the curtain, and light up cigarettes.

Yes, the cast members in this act, in which lung control was very important, were big smokers. Most were from Ireland, Russia, and Czechoslovakia, where smoking is rampant. (It's now banned in Irish pubs; I can't imagine how they're getting along.)

So, away they puffed, like little chimneys. They went through forty packs of cigarettes a day; that's what was provided to them by the company. A little corollary to the usual axiom: In this case, where there's smoke, there's fiery footwork.

LEND ME THREE TENORS— AND SUITS AND AIR FARE

It's not enough just to put on productions today. Dallas Summer Musicals is actively training tomorrow's talent with a Dallas Summer Musicals School. We occasionally stage benefits for this school, and on a plane to New York one day I was thinking of what we might do to raise money.

I thought of the popular "Three Tenors" touring show, but of course, this show, featuring the world's greatest tenors, was enormously expensive—a quarter of a million dollars for an hour and a half—and was totally out of the realm of possibility.

150

Still, I tweaked and picked at this idea, and by the time I arrived in a taxi at the New York office of a talent agency I had an idea. I asked the agent to find me the three best tenors on Broadway.

As we were discussing the idea, he asked if I'd go next door with him and meet some people who'd come to see him from something I understood to be Bee-el-kee. I didn't know any Bee-el-kee, but I said OK. We went to the meeting, and the people turned out to be from Brioni, the suit manufacturer. As luck would have it, I was wearing a Brioni sport coat, which started things out on a nice note.

I mentioned the Three Broadway Tenors plan, and the suit guy immediately pounced on it: Why not put the tenors in Brioni suits: one blue, one gray, and one beige. He'd provide the suits.

I liked that idea, especially the part about their being provided free.

On the way home on the airplane, I sat next to Al Casey, who at the time was chairman of American Airlines. He asked what I was up to. I told him about the Three Broadway Tenors, and he suggested that American Airlines fly them—free, of course—to Dallas and put them up at a downtown hotel. I liked that idea very much, too.

Some trips turn out to be so profitable! We were able to have Three Broadway Tenors in three Brioni suits flown to Dallas and put up in a hotel. They performed at the Adam's Mark Hotel, and the proceeds—which didn't have to be diverted to expenses such as clothes and plane tickets—went to our school and the Dallas Business Committee for the Arts.

How's that for a happy ending?

CHAPTER TEN:

THE WALLS HAVE EARS, AND SO DO I

This is a love story. And it's not mine. It's just one I couldn't help knowing about.

I was traveling in Australia with my friend whom I'll call Arthur (not his real name). We'd stopped for a night on the Gold Coast, where Arthur knew a woman who designed string bikinis. He was very much in love with her, so he often came to the Gold Coast to be with her. We all had dinner together.

Later that evening, after I'd gone to bed, I learned exactly how much Arthur loved the woman and the woman loved Arthur—thanks to the fact that our hotel had paper-thin walls.

"Ohhhh, Arthur, Arthur," she moaned for what seemed like hours. I finally picked up the telephone and called the room next door.

"Arthur," I said, "will you please finish so we can

152

all go to sleep?" I was hoping for a laugh, but the fact was that it was getting late and I was, indeed, ready to call it a night.

The room next door suddenly became completely quiet. And so were Arthur and his friend the next morning at breakfast—completely quiet. I didn't ask if they had slept well, and they didn't ask me, either.

HIGH NOON

It's hard to disguise a Texas accent, and I have one. So does Ron Shook, director of planning at LARC. So we're used to people calling us "Tex" and giving us a hard time about the way we talk.

One day Ron and I were in a taxi in Sydney, Australia, and the driver, noticing that we didn't talk like Australians (to put it mildly), asked where we were from.

"Texas," I said.

He screeched over to the side of the road, stopped the car, turned around, and asked us if we had any guns.

"If you have any guns," he said, "you'll have to put them out of the taxi. I don't allow guns."

We assured him we didn't have any guns. He looked dubious.

"I thought everyone in Texas had guns," he said. We assured him that was not the case, and in any event, the two of us weren't packing heat.

He drove on, but he kept an eye on us in the rearview mirror. Never know when one of those trigger-happy Texans will decide to start blasting away. *Yee haw!*

TALE OF THE SUGAR SMUGGLER

Sometimes you have to just sneak off to foreign countries so that people don't ask you to bring them back things. I'm always one to say "no problem" when somebody asks a favor. Trouble is, you never know exactly how much of a problem a favor might turn out to be.

After an extremely arduous month-long trip to Australia, I called home before I left to ask if anybody needed anything from Australia. I was asked to bring castor sugar. It's a very finely ground sugar used in making Pavlova, the national dessert of Australia.

So I went to a store. Unfortunately, this store was out of castor sugar except for one box that had a hole in it. The tiny granules were escaping, though not much had made it out yet. The store owner offered to pour the sugar into a Zip-loc bag for me.

Fine, I said, and made the purchase. Back at my hotel, I wrapped a shirt around the Zip-loc bag and tossed the sugar into my suitcase.

You've already figured out what happened, right? When I arrived in Hawaii and went through customs, they opened my bags and there was a nice Zip-loc bag full of white powder peeking out. What were the customs guys supposed to think? Cocaine!

They took it off to be tested, and, of course, I missed my connection back home. The customs guys finally finished their test and came to the unhappy conclusion that this dumb American was, in fact, carrying a bag of sugar.

When I arrived back home—a day late—the sugar

was the first thing out of my suitcase, accompanied by a lament about how much trouble it had caused.

"I don't really need it now," I was told. "I just put some regular sugar in a Cuisinart."

AH, THE BEAUTY OF SYDNEY

Sydney, Australia, is an awesome city. I didn't know how awesome until a friend of mine decided to take me sailing in Sydney Harbor on his boat one lovely afternoon.

His boat was quite large. I didn't know anything about sailing, but I was enjoying the beautiful day and the brisk breeze.

My friend handed me some binoculars.

"Look down the beach to your right," he suggested and I did. Goodness! A nude beach! It was Lady Jane Beach, known for its clothing-optional policies.

As I was taking in these sights, the wind shifted and the sailboat's boom swung around and caught me right in the midsection, swinging me, with it, over the side of the boat, where I dangled precariously over the water.

Everyone on the boat began to work feverishly to pull the boom—and me—back over the deck, but it was quite a chore because of the intense wind.

Finally, they got me back in the boat. But I'd like to note that I did not drop the binoculars. No, I held them tight the whole time.

And I will remember that as the day I learned how wonderful and beautiful Australia really was. Particularly the beaches.

IT'S A SMALL WORLD AFTER ALL

I had to make an emergency trip to Australia. The emergency wasn't mine; it was the emergency of Charles Curran, a friend who at the time owned the State Theatre on Union Street in Sydney, a theatre similar to Dallas' Majestic Theatre.

Charles had a major, major problem to resolve and needed me to fly to Australia immediately. I dropped everything and showed up. Keep in mind that it's impossible to show up in Australia from the United States "immediately." It takes two days to get there. So by the time I showed up, Charles was just days from the deadline by which he had to solve this problem.

But show up I did, as quickly as possible, arriving at 6:30 A.M. By 7:30 P.M. we had resolved his problem and were off to dinner. He took me to a new restaurant—one of those that revolved atop Centrepoint, a tall tower in Sydney. It was a good restaurant, although the tables were very close together.

After the meal, he wanted to show me the observation deck. When I pulled out my chair to get up, I bumped into the guy behind me, who was facing the opposite direction. I turned to apologize and saw none other than my next-door neighbor in Dallas, dining with a lovely Australian woman.

"Guess you'll have to mow my yard now," I joked. He laughed nervously.

Some months later on a Saturday morning, my daughter, Tiffany, came flying out into the living room. "Dad!" she yelled. "Mr. Jones is mowing our yard. Why?"

"Because he's a very nice man," I said, and no one spoke of the subject again.

IT'S ABE—HONEST

The first day I met Abe Saffron, he came to my Dallas LARC office with Hal and Col Goldstein to talk about redevelopment of Luna Park, a well-known park in Sydney Harbor in Australia.

It was summer in Dallas—a miserable time of the year, weather-wise. We were all dying in 100-degree heat. In walked Abe Saffron in a hat and very long wool overcoat. I asked him if he'd like to take the coat off and hang it up. No, he said.

We met in the conference room for about four hours, with Abe in his heavy coat the whole time. We took the three men to the airport after the meeting, and they flew back to Australia.

During work on the park, LARC's director of planning, Ron Shook, and I flew to Sydney, clearing customs at around 7:30 A.M. Col Goldstein took us to breakfast on Williams Street in the heart of Sydney. As Col dropped Ron and me off to go park the car, we saw a man in a long overcoat walking a dog. It was Abe Saffron. We spoke to him and he said, "Hello, I heard you were coming. Glad you're here." And he kept walking.

We went inside and ordered coffee. When Col came in, we told him we'd just seen Abe Saffron outside, walking his dog.

"No you didn't," he said.

"Yeah, we did," I said. "We talked to him."

"No you didn't. He's not here. He's in Israel."

After breakfast, we got into the car, and as we drove down Williams Street, there was the man in the long overcoat. I waved to him, and he waved back.

157

"Look!" I said to Col. "There he is! It's Abe!"

"Abe who?" Col asked.

"Abe Saffron! There!"

"Abe Saffron," he proclaimed, "is in Israel." This despite the conclusive evidence of our eyes.

It was much later that I learned that while Abe Saffron—a well-known character often called "colorful" in the Australian press—was often a helpful man to know, he was not always a man to acknowledge knowing. Or even seeing. But we at LARC always knew Abe Saffron when we saw him.

MONSTERS!

Halloween is a big holiday in the United States, but it took a while before it became popular in Australia. I happened to be in Perth on the first year the Australians really got into the holiday.

It was October 31. "The Great Pumpkin" was on TV. Folks were eating candy corn. Australia was getting into a real Halloween mood.

Ron Shook and I had dinner then went to the bar for a drink. Ron decided to stay there, but I opted to walk back to our hotel about six blocks away.

It was 1:30 A.M., and the streets were deserted. The street I was walking on went down a hill, dipping low into a foggy area. As I walked along, I stopped at a red light—then wondered why there wasn't a soul around.

Suddenly, I looked to my right and saw, emerging from the fog at the bottom of the hill, Dracula. He walked slowly up the hill.

Stunned, I stood completely silent.

He walked up to me and said in a distinct Transylvanian accent, "Good *eeeeeeeevening*." Then he walked on across the street.

Run!

Seized by a sudden panic, I impulsively began to run. I beat it all the way back to the hotel and, four blocks later, arrived panting. Ron, when he saw me later, said I looked like a ghost.

Please, I begged: Let's not talk about ghosts. I'd just seen a monster.

I'd let my imagination get the best of me. It was not, of course, really Dracula. It was a guy on his way to or from a Halloween costume party. Of course it was.

WHINE OF THE DAY

Let me tell you about the best bottle of wine I never had.

When I was traveling in Australia, Ron Shook and I went to Bribie Island in Queensland to meet a fellow named Albert Hedger. Mr. Hedger took us to see the constable, a real VIP of the region who happened to be a true wine connoisseur. We had a long conversation about wine with the constable—as if we knew anything about wine—and he seemed to enjoy talking with a couple of Texans. He'd never met a Texan before and, well, you know how people are.

At the end of our conversation he gifted us with a bottle of rare wine. In fact, the constable thought there were only two bottles of it in existence. Of course we greatly appreciated his gesture, so to keep the wine safe we wrapped it in a cloth and placed it gently on the floor of the back seat of our car.

We drove to two other destinations, then as Ron opened the back door, the bottle of rare wine fell out and crashed to the pavement. We watched it literally run down the drain into a gutter. We stood there in amazement, in total shock, and begged Albert Hedger never to tell the constable what happened to the bottle.

We couldn't believe the bottle had somehow rolled itself over the big hump on the floor to the other side of the car. Of course, we never got a taste of that fabulous Australian wine, and we left in fear that the constable would find out what happened. Please keep our little secret.

The Ferris wheel at Sydney's Luna Park.

Welcome to Sydney, Australia's Luna Park.

CHAPTER ELEVEN:

IT'S A MIRACLE!

The Phantom of the Opera is a wildly popular musical, and anywhere it plays, all kinds of people come out to see it.

All kinds.

One evening during a run of *Phantom* at Dallas Summer Musicals, a woman in a wheelchair arrived for an evening performance. The ushers rolled her to the section of the auditorium dedicated to audience members in wheelchairs.

She was not happy. This, she said, was not where she thought the people in wheelchairs sat. She thought people in wheelchairs were placed very close to the stage.

No, she was politely informed, this is where the wheelchairs always are.

She demanded to speak with the manager. An usher came to my office and retrieved me, and I talked to the woman, explaining as courteously as I could that this was, indeed, where the wheelchairs always sat.

It finally occurred to her that I might be telling the truth, whereupon she opened her purse and pulled out a ticket to the show.

"My seats are better than these," she announced.

And lo, she arose from her wheelchair and walked— all the way down the aisle to the seat listed on the ticket, where she sat down and watched the performance.

The usher could only shake his head as he rolled the empty wheelchair back to the lobby.

OH, PIPE DOWN!

One night at the Music Hall a woman who identified herself as a season ticket-holder asked to see me. Nothing unusual there.

When I arrived, she complained that the woman behind her kept singing along with the performers on stage. Could I come down and stop her from singing?

Oh, boy. Why don't we just transform the Music Hall into a giant karaoke bar and be done with it?

But I dutifully went down, met the lady in question, and asked, "Are you the lady who sings?"

She said, "Yes, and I'm quite good."

I said, "I'm sure that you're wonderful, but these people sitting around you actually paid to hear someone else sing. I'm afraid you'll have to be quiet during the performance."

She said, "Oh no, I've been rehearsing all week. I know all the songs and I WILL be singing. It'll be great—like stereo."

164

I had a handwritten petition in my hand signed by six people sitting around her: All of these patrons demanded the woman should stop singing. But I didn't want to pull out that petition, and, for that matter, I didn't want to tell the woman to put a sock in it.

I told her she was more than welcome to continue singing—you should have seen the frowns on the faces of the other patrons when I said this—but first she would have to follow me. I told her we had a wonderful video screen with a camera in the lobby for those who arrive late. I said she was welcome to sit there, outside the auditorium, and sing.

Believe it or not, she said this was a grand idea.

So I escorted her up the aisle to the lobby. We turned around a couch and a chair to face the screen, and I brought the woman a complimentary soft drink. All this to keep her in the lobby and away from those half-dozen annoyed subscribers.

We lowered the screen, turned on the camera, and sure enough, it was a wonderful picture. I left to attend to other business, and when I came back I heard her singing at the top of her lungs. And darned if she wasn't pretty good.

No one inside the auditorium could hear her, but at the end of her performance in the lobby, all the bartenders and maintenance personnel gave her a big hand. I think that's all she needed in the first place.

SICK MAN WALKING

Most people go straight to bed when they're sick.

Others feel the need to visit the hospital. We've got a guy who comes straight to the Music Hall.

One night before the show, he came up to me and said he didn't think he'd live through the performance. I said, "Hey, I've seen the show. It's not that bad ..."

He missed the joke entirely. "No, no. I really don't feel well," he said.

This is a man who comes to almost every show, and there's something wrong with him virtually every time.

His nose is bleeding. He was scalded by hot water in the men's room. Whatever.

On this particular night, he looked intently at me and said, "If anything happens to me—do this!" He dramatically grabbed my wrist and jammed a folded-up note in my hand. Then he turned and strode straight into the theatre.

When he'd found his seat once again, and I felt safe to breathe again, I opened the note.

It read, "Call 911!"

This is a most bizarre man, but we always enjoy him arriving at our door. There's always some crisis in his life and, let's face it, drama makes the day go faster.

DALLAS: WHERE'S THE BEEF?

I saw this same man, the hypochondriac, hovering near our Music Hall restaurant during one Sunday evening performance.

He tried to be surreptitious, but virtually everyone saw him pick up a large slab of roast beef and put it in his pocket. The restaurant people went wild, of course,

166

because he hadn't paid for it. No one could believe this man had just picked up a slice of beef with his bare hands and walked out.

Would you care for some horseradish, sir? A little au jus, perhaps?

When I approached the man he confounded me with his own, twisted logic. "Well, it's not going to be eaten, anyway," he began. "You're going to have to throw it out because there's no performance tomorrow. So, why don't you just let me eat it?"

When I told him that was not going to happen, he claimed that he didn't even have the slice of beef.

Huh?

I pointed to a widening stain on his pants. "Then what's that blood and grease staining your pants?" I wanted to know.

That's when he pulled out the slab and took a big bite of it. He said it wasn't that good anyway, and handed it back to me. Go figure: A moment ago he was a petty thief. Now he's a food critic.

Of course, the last thing I wanted was to touch this beef that had been in his pocket and now had a bite out of it. I felt like a principal demanding the bubble gum of a misbehaving student, then wondering how I wound up with a wet piece of chewed gum in my hand.

CATS FIGHT

As it turns out, nine lives aren't nearly enough.

To date, Atlanta has mounted fifteen productions of the musical blockbuster *Cats* with no letup in sight. As of this writing, the Dallas Summer Musicals has brought the Andrew Lloyd Webber show to town four times, so we're in the sweepstakes, too.

I'm neither bragging nor apologizing. The facts are these: Bring up the curtain on *Cats* and you've got a winner. Do it in the summer, do it in the winter, do it in the nude—the show always sells.

I mention this because *Cats* was a sore spot with a certain formidable but ultimately gracious Dallas socialite named Harriet Rose. She turned out to be a good friend and someone we've all missed since her death a few years ago.

Sometimes I'm not so sure she's gone. Less than a year after she died, her Maple Avenue apartment caught fire. Some folks speculated it was just Harriet still blazing away.

The day I met her, years ago, I was new on the scene. Harriet came up to me in a restaurant as I was waiting for Wendy to arrive for lunch.

"Young man," she said. "Aren't you Michael Jenkins?"

Harriet Rose was a short, somewhat elderly woman but she was intimidating when she wanted to be.

I said, "Yes, and I know who you are. You're Harriet Rose, and it's a pleasure to finally meet you."

She didn't beat around the bush with pleasantries. "You see this umbrella?" she said. (It was a full-sized model with a thick wooden handle, not a dainty woman's parasol.)

I said, "Yes."

She said, "Well, if you ever bring *Cats* back to Dallas again, I'm going to beat you senseless with this umbrella. Do you understand?"

I chickened out right there. I lamely mumbled, "Yes, ma'am. Thank you very much." Something like that.

She went back to her table and sat down as she awaited a friend. After that, I was afraid to so much as look in her direction. The fact that I'd signed a contract to bring *Cats* to Dallas only a week earlier left me feeling gutless.

I hadn't the nerve to tell her the dreaded news.

Harriet's friend arrived and they began chatting. I overheard Harriet tell her, "That man over there is Michael Jenkins, and I just told him exactly what I would do to him if he ever brought *Cats* back to the Music Hall."

Suddenly, I could see myself being publicly flogged by this short lady with a big umbrella. Since I hadn't spoken up when I had the chance, I'd just have to stand there and take it.

As it turned out, Harriet's friend happened to love *Cats*, and the two of them got into an animated debate over the show. They even tried to drag me into the controversy, but I wasn't about to referee. Mercifully, the maitre d' arrived and ushered me into the bar area just to get me out of the line of fire.

Later, this little story was written up in *Newsweek*. There's a framed copy in my office, although I'll never know how the story wound up in the magazine. Still, it's a fond reminder of my *Cats*-hating, umbrella-wielding friend, Harriet Rose, whom I came to greatly admire.

Incidentally, about those two friends arguing the show's merits in a restaurant: That's the way it is with *Cats*. You love it or you hate it. There's no middle ground.

Either way, the show must go on. And on and on. The Dallas Summer Musicals is partners with Troika Entertainment, the organization with touring rights to

the long-running hit. So, yes, you'll see it again. The famous marketing pitch is *"Cats*—Now and Forever."
You'd better believe that's more than just a slogan.

MASTER OF THE SEAT

Where better to play musical chairs than the Music Hall?

We've got a Thursday matinee patron—Code Name "Johnny G"—who keeps trying for an upgrade. Trying and failing, I might add. He buys a ticket for the balcony and spends most of the first act scoping out the seats below in the orchestra section.

I think his only goal in coming to the theatre is to sneak down from the balcony to an empty orchestra seat without detection. The man is obsessed. Of course, we always find him and escort him out.

It's not like you can't see him coming a mile away. He's always dressed in the same get-up: beige sports coat, blue jeans and white tennis shoes. And he carries a strange wooden briefcase. Inside, there's apparently nothing but a yellow writing tablet and a No. 2 pencil.

Each time we catch him trying to sneak into an orchestra seat, he always says the same thing as we lead him away. He says, "Next Thursday you guys won't be able to find me."

How on earth could we miss him?

But keep trying, fella. You keep us on our toes.

A HEARTY PERFORMANCE

Audience members would be so much better off if

they'd leave the acting to the folks on-stage. But it doesn't always happen that way.

Before a 2:OO P.M. Sunday matinee, a woman came up to me and proclaimed that her husband had recently had a heart operation. They were sitting in the balcony. She wondered: Might they be moved to the orchestra level because of her husband's recent operation?

"How recent?" I asked.

"This morning," she answered.

I asked her where this heart operation had taken place, and she told me it had been performed at Baylor Hospital in Dallas. He'd had the operation, then they'd raced off so as not to miss the matinee for which they had tickets.

Hmmm. I happened to know Baylor Hospital pretty well. I'd had heart operations there, in fact—an angioplasty, a roto-rooter type thing to unclog my arteries, and two stent implants. But I'd never had a heart operation in the morning and been released to frolic around the Music Hall in the afternoon. This one-act play's plot was a little thin.

I asked to see the woman's tickets. What she didn't know was that the tickets are coded, so I could see when and where they'd been purchased—at 4:30 the day before at our box office on Berkshire Lane.

"When did you buy these?" I asked.

"I don't recall," she answered.

I refreshed her memory: It had been yesterday.

She looked me straight in the eye and said, "You're not going to let me move to the orchestra section, are you?"

"That's correct," I replied.

"Well," she said, turning around, "thought I'd try."
And she walked off. End of one-act play.

NEVER MIND

I'm not going to say that some of our Dallas
Summer Musicals guests aren't the sharpest knives in
the drawer, or that a few of them seem to be a few
tacos short of a Number 2 dinner. I'm not going to say
that. I'm just going to tell this story.

When we did *Aida*, a woman called me, all upset.
Why on earth was I having *Evita* back? We'd just done
Evita recently.

"It's not *Evita*," I explained. "It's *Aida*."

"Yes, *Evita*," she said. "I know. I've seen the show
before. It's about Eva Peron. Why would you bring this
back?"

I was unable to convince her that *Aida* was a different show.

Another woman wanted to know if the show was a
benefit for AIDS research.

My phone calls are never boring.

OUT FOR A SATURDAY DRIVE

A man arrived at one Saturday matinee in a most
spectacular way.

He came careening through the parking lot, nearly
running down a security guard and knocking three
signs over, then jumped the curb, drove up the Music
Hall's walkway, and parked on the steps.

He emerged from the car.

The security staff and I were there to greet him. We'd seen his little performance and were not at all amused. We informed him that it was unacceptable to drive recklessly through the parking lot, endangering lives, and that he could not park on the Music Hall steps.

He said for the price of his ticket, he could park anywhere he wanted.

A debate on this question ensued, and security got some background from the driver: He and his wife had had an argument on the way to the Music Hall about that particular show. He'd put her out at a red light four blocks from the Music Hall and vented his wrath in the parking lot before arriving on our front steps.

His wife soon arrived, huffing and puffing. She was even madder than he was. And she had the tickets. She made him apologize before she'd give him his ticket. They went in to see the show, and I heard nothing more from them.

Apparently, she wasn't one to hold a grudge.

FIELD GOAL!

At the Music Hall at Fair Park, the action is supposed to take place on the stage. But often, there's plenty of drama in the audience.

One night a man and woman who were dressed extremely well—almost overdressed, actually—arrived at the Music Hall, and I saw them pass as I was standing in the auditorium.

I heard the woman remark, "Next time I say I want a Coke, I want a Coca-Cola."

The man replied that she would have water. Water was what she would have.

They argued all the way down the aisle to their seats—Section C, Row C (third row) on the aisle.

The beautifully dressed woman had a lovely purse with a long strap. I don't know if the purse fell or she put it down or what, but the next thing I knew, her companion had picked up the purse from the floor and drop-kicked it like a football completely across the theatre, where it landed in Section E, Row S.

This happened to be near the end of the first act of *The Phantom of the Opera*, when the chandelier falls. All eyes are on the chandelier, normally. This time, 3,000 heads were turned to follow the purse in its descent, which was far more dramatic than that of the chandelier.

I went racing across the auditorium to retrieve the purse, grateful it hadn't caused any injury, and during intermission I went down to have a discussion with this couple. I told them that if they couldn't behave, we'd have to remove them from the theatre.

Neither wanted to sit next to the other for the second act. But it was a sold-out show; there was no place to which either squabbler might be moved. I informed them they would have to stay put, but if there was a single problem, they'd be gone. I positioned an usher to keep an eye on the situation, and back in my office, I periodically watched a monitor to check on them. I couldn't see anything going on.

At the end of the performance, I was standing in

the lobby and saw the man and woman emerge. They were holding hands, almost skipping with joy.

They walked up to me and said the second act of *Phantom* had changed their life. I was dumbfounded. In the second act of *Phantom* the heroine gets imprisoned by a crazy fiend in an opera house. It's not really very romantic.

I've watched this musical again and again, thinking of this couple. I still can't figure out what moved them to reconcile.

MANY UNHAPPY RETURNS

I don't know why I'm telling this story, it's so awful. But I promised the good, the bad, and the ugly, so here goes:

An anniversary couple came to one of our productions for their big evening, and they looked to be having a grand time. The gentleman had bought his wife a beautiful sequined gown of three-quarters length, and she looked splendid. He wore a stylish new suit.

They ate in our restaurant, and by pre-arrangement there was a special anniversary emblem on the table and a red rose at her chair. Everything was going so well—at least until the couple went to their seats to watch *Riverdance*.

Unfortunately, the woman wound up sitting right next to an Irishman who was very deeply in his cups. At some point in the first act, the man became ill and— I don't know any nice way to say it—he threw up all over the lady in her new sequined gown.

It was a horrible scene, simply indescribable.

We took responsibility for cleaning the woman's dress, but after two dry-cleanings, it was clear the dress was totally ruined. The husband held us responsible. He said it was our fault for seating a man next to them in that condition.

Our view was that with 3,400 people in the theatre that night, we couldn't possibly know the drinking habits of every person entering the auditorium. We invited the couple back to another production and did all we could to make things better, but the whole business was never resolved to their satisfaction.

I felt terrible, but sometimes all you can do is still not good enough.

As for the man who had too much to drink, I heard later that he seemed to feel better after getting sick. Acting as though nothing had happened, he stayed for the rest of the show, cheering the Irish dancers and seeming to enjoy himself immensely.

HOW TO SUCCEED IN CONFUSING PEOPLE

How to Succeed in Business Without Really Trying is, of course, the name of a Broadway show, and this particular year we'd booked it at Dallas Summer Musicals.

As the advertisements for it began to appear, I got a strange phone call. A woman asked me what time the business seminar was.

"What business seminar?" I asked.

"The one on how to succeed in business without trying very hard," she said. I had to explain to her that there was no seminar offered on that topic—though if there were, I think I'd sign up for it, too.

TRAGEDY TONIGHT

This really is a sad story. What's good is that it only happened once—that I know of.

During a run of *The Phantom of the Opera*, a young woman came to buy tickets. She was ecstatic: The boyfriend with whom she'd recently broken up had returned to town to see her. They were planning to see *Phantom*.

On that night, her boyfriend drove to the Music Hall at Fair Park but had trouble finding a parking place, because the State Fair of Texas was in town. So he dropped her off at the theatre, telling her to go into the theatre restaurant and order for both of them; he'd be right in.

She came in and ordered. Half an hour later, he had not come in. We urged her to go ahead and eat, because curtain time was near. She finally did eat, then waited for him to come in with the tickets.

At curtain time, he hadn't arrived. We found a spot for her to sit and assured her that when the young man arrived, we would take him to where she was seated.

At intermission, he had not arrived.

By the end of the performance, he still had not arrived. She kept waiting; after all, she had arrived in his vehicle.

At 2:30 A.M., even she was certain that he was not going to return. I hated to leave her there, so I had one of our staff people take her to her home, which was quite some distance from the Music Hall.

The next day, she reported him missing. Three days later, his car was found parked at a motel in Waco. He was inside with another girlfriend.

Phantom will always have special meaning to that young lady—unfortunately, not a good one.

WHAT A DRAG

One thing about producing shows in Texas: There's a strong contingent of folks who see themselves as moral guardians of the young. And they're quite strict about what they want kids to see and not see.

You wouldn't think they'd have trouble with a production of *Cinderella*. You would be wrong.

During a 2000 production of *Cinderella* starring Eartha Kitt, the role of one of the stepmothers was played by a man.

A woman and a man called me on the phone, both saying that I was out to subvert the morals of Dallas schoolchildren. I let them know that this was a touring show that I had not cast; I didn't know that the stepmother was a guy in drag until the show arrived (and, for that matter, he did a great job in the role).

Still, these people were angry, and angry they would stay.

Too bad you can't just wave a wand . . .

TAKEN TO TASKING

Those of you who can walk and chew gum at the same time are to be congratulated. You've been multitasking all along and didn't even know it.

The experts say that watching TV while eating is a form of multi-tasking, so give yourself credit for all those hours spent snacking in front of the tube. Almost 25 percent of Americans can't eat unless they're doing another activity along with it. Which goes a long way in explaining some of the, uh, multi-taskers who visit the Music Hall.

Now we have a word for them. I never knew before what to call them.

Several years ago a woman came up to me at intermission and complained about two ladies in front of her who were eating potato chips during the show.

Oh, please.

I went to the row in question and discovered empty potato chip bags on the floor. When the women returned following intermission, I discreetly informed them they couldn't eat any more potato chips during the performance. They must have thought they were at the movies. They wanted to know why they couldn't eat potato chips. I explained that their snacking was disturbing the patrons around them. Finally, I got them to promise they wouldn't eat any more potato chips.

Yet as I was leaving, I saw one of the women reach into her purse and withdraw something.

"It's OK," she said triumphantly. "These are Doritos."

CHAPTER TWELVE:

INN TROUBLE

It was a cold, rainy afternoon when I arrived in Nashua, New Hampshire, for a meeting with Arthur Provencher, at that time the owner of Benson's Wild Animal Farm, a business he'd started with a lame elephant from a circus.

He had made me a reservation at a small 1930s-era motel with individual cabins. It was called the White Horse Inn, and it is among my most memorable accommodations.

The taxi dropped me off in a torrential rainstorm. In the lobby, on the desk telephone, was a guy who looked like Mel of Mel's Diner in *Alice*. Or maybe a longshoreman. He had a big anchor tattoo on his arm.

The guy was chatting with his wife about what they should have for dinner. Potatoes? Green beans? Or maybe they should save the green beans for another day.

This went on for quite some time, until I finally asked to check in. He asked his wife to hold for a moment, threw a key at me and said, "Building 6." It was, of course, the farthest from the check-in office.

"Do you have an umbrella?" I asked. No, he said, but he gave me a box to put over my head.

So, box over head, briefcase and hanging bag in arms, out I went into the storm, making my way to Building 6, which stretched the definition of the word "building." It was about the size of a single-car garage and was devoid of decorative touches. Still, it was dry.

I laid my clothes on the bed so I could make an important phone call. I searched high and low: no phone.

I grabbed the box, put it back over my head, and trudged back to the office, where the guy with the tattoo was still in heavy dinner discussions. Up for debate was the question of whether to have fish or pork chops.

I asked if there was a phone I might use. He again asked his wife to hold and, exasperated, told me the only phone was a pay phone out on the pole. He did notice that my box was falling apart, and he said I could have another one. Sweet guy. So I took it and headed out to the telephone pole, where I made my call and dashed back to Building 6.

May as well hang up my clothes, I thought—then discovered there was no closet. There were no hangers. There was no place for clothes to be.

Back went the box over my head, and I sloshed back to the office, where, of course, the guy was still on the phone arguing the merits of garden salad versus Jell-O. Extremely irritated, he blurted, "What now?"

"I wonder," I said, "if there might be a closet."

"You want a closet?" he asked.

"Well . . . somewhere to hang up my clothes," I suggested.

"Go back to the room," he said. "I'll be there when I finish this call."

On the trudge back to the room, I wondered whether the call would ever be finished. And I wondered if I really wanted this man to come to Building 6.

But come down he did. I saw him charging down the walkway—with an umbrella over his head, I'd like to note. He was carrying a hammer. He came roaring through the door and asked, "Where do you want that closet?"

"Well . . . anywhere," I said. "Here is fine."

He took a 16-penny nail out of his pocket and with the hammer pounded it into the wall a few times. Then he threw a few hangers on the bed and said, "There's your closet!" and left.

I wasn't about to ask him for anything else. Like soap.

THE BIG ORANGE IN THE BIG APPLE

In late 1963, when Angus Wynne, Jr., was building the Texas pavilion at the World's Fair in New York, I was sent up to be in charge of personnel for shows and to serve as assistant general manager for the pavilion.

Unbeknownst to me, Mr. Wynne had met with the

famous artist Josef Albers, who is known for painting large, bright-colored squares. Mr. Wynne hired Albers to paint a mural on the side of the pavilion.

A few days later, my secretary came in and said, "I didn't know we were having an Orange Julius in the building."

"We're not," I said.

"Well, they're painting a big Orange Julius sign on the side of the building," she replied.

I rushed out and went down the elevator to check, and sure enough: There was scaffolding on the building, and large orange squares were being painted. I soon learned that this was not an Orange Julius sign, but a work of art.

Sometimes it's hard to tell with these modern painters. Their art belongs to Dada.

BIG BIRD AND FRIENDS

I'm not an easily surprised person. That comes from years of seeing the unexpected.

Take, for example, the time colleague Ron Shook and I traveled to Asheville, North Carolina, to meet a gentleman who raised miniature horses and wanted to develop a tourist attraction around them.

It was the dead of winter—bitter cold—and our plane had had trouble landing, but we'd arrived and traveled out to the farm, where the man invited us in for a hot cup of coffee, noting that his wife was out of town.

It was one of those shotgun-type houses with a hall down the middle with rooms on each side. We were sitting in a living room at the front of the house, with the hall behind us. Our host, Mark, had gone into the kitchen to make coffee.

Noticing movement out of the corner of my eye, I looked back into the hall and saw an ostrich. Nah, couldn't be an ostrich.

I looked over at Ron. He, too, had seen the ostrich. We looked dumbfounded at each other.

I called out to Mark that I really hated to bother him, but that I thought there was an ostrich in the house.

"Oh, yeah," he said, "that's Dolly." He explained that he felt it was too cold for the bird to stay outside, and since his wife was out of town, he saw no harm in allowing the bird—which was nearly as tall as the ceiling—to stay in the house.

Ron and I left, shaking our heads, certain that Mark had quite a cleanup job ahead of him before his wife got home.

PAAAAAHHKING THE CAHHHHHH

One of our longtime clients, Arthur Provencher, who owned Benson's Animal Park in Nashua, New Hampshire, came to Dallas to see me. He was very excited; for my fortieth birthday, he was bringing me a hand-carved model circus wagon I'd admired for years in his collection.

In a huge rush at Boston's Logan International Airport, he pulled up to the curb in front of the airport, got out, and made sure the porter correctly handled the box containing my circus wagon. He dashed off to get on the plane and flew to Dallas.

184

We were in the middle of dinner when he suddenly threw down his knife and fork and said, "Oh, gosh! I left my car running in front of the airport!"

The next morning, we checked with security and police, who had found the car (or the *cahhhhh*, as Bostonians always pronounce it) idling away in front of the airport. They'd taken it to a secure lot and parked it until Arthur could return to get it.

Later, Arthur reported back gleefully that when he'd arrived back in Boston, he'd found his car in the lost-and-found car lot. (Apparently there are a lot of cars that are lost and found.) Getting the car freed from this lot actually cost less than if he'd parked the car in a legitimate space at Logan.

He was seriously considering leaving his car running in front of the airport again next time.

HAND ME THAT TRUNK

Arthur Provencher started Benson's Animal Farm with a circus elephant he'd rescued on its way to euthanasia. He loved that elephant. He loved all elephants. He spent a lot of time learning about all things pachyderm.

One of the things that he learned was that in any representation of an elephant, if the trunk was down, it would bring bad luck. The trunk on an elephant should always be raised in any drawing or statue of the beast.

While we were developing Benson's Animal Park, Arthur came to take a look. In the park, there was a fine marble statue of an elephant—fine in every way except that, Arthur noticed immediately, the trunk was pointed down.

Arthur gathered the park's employees and made a huge show of knocking the trunk off the elephant with a sledgehammer. He broke it into itty bitty pieces so that it could not be glued back on. Everyone was horrified. It may have been only a marble elephant, but the act seemed so . . . violent. But Arthur explained: Elephant trunks must always be up, to avoid bad luck.

A month later, back in Dallas, I received a very heavy package in the mail. Sure enough, Arthur had mailed me that trunk—in pieces. He wanted to make sure I got the message: No southward-pointing trunks. Ever.

I got the message, and any elephant statue we've done for any venue anywhere in the world since has had its trunk held high over its head. I have a long memory too.

CALL ME A CAB—BUT NOT THAT ONE

On another cold, snowy night—why do I always seem to travel on those?—Ron Shook and I flew to Detroit, arriving on the last flight to that city from Dallas at about 12:30 A.M. in a blizzard. It was the kind where snow blows sideways. No fun for two Texans.

We were the first ones off the plane and hadn't checked baggage, which turned out to be a good thing, because at that hour of the morning, there aren't many taxis lurking around the airport. There was one in sight. We hailed it.

The driver jumped out, and we immediately perceived that he had not bathed for several weeks. He opened the trunk and threw our bags in. Too late, we noticed the still-dripping oil cans he'd obviously used recently to service his taxi. There were our bags, in the midst of a huge oil slick. We sighed and got in the cab.

Once we'd entered the taxi, we realized our earlier estimates on the timing of the driver's last bath were probably too conservative. He also cranked up the heat as we drove along, and the combination of factors led us to roll down the windows and drink in the blizzard.

We arrived at our hotel at 1:15 A.M. and spent the next hour and a half cleaning the oil off our bags, vowing to check on the condition of a taxi in the future before getting in it.

Two and a half months later, we found ourselves flying into Detroit again. Once again, when we emerged from the Detroit airport, taxis were in short supply. One stopped, and we grabbed it. The driver got out and popped the trunk.

With no small degree of horror, we realized it was the same guy! Still, we couldn't see any other taxis around, so . . . we asked if we could keep our luggage inside the cab.

No, he said, that would cause a weight problem, and we couldn't use the front seat because it was full of newspapers.

We asked if we could put some of the newspapers in the trunk to protect our bags from the oil.

The driver got huffy. Curling his lip, he said that any real man would throw his bags in the trunk and get going. We replied that we were real men, and we had already thrown our bags in his trunk once before. That's why we wanted newspapers put down.

We were soon off in the cab, windows rolled down, our bags in the trunk without any newspapers beneath them.

We arrived at the hotel and spent the next hour and a half cleaning our bags.

Ron and I resolved to simply realize that when we came to Motor City we'd have to clean motor oil off our bags. Either that or just leave them grimy and proclaim ourselves wealthy Texas oilmen.

COME ONE, COME ALL

When LARC was in the process of designing the Kentucky Kingdom theme park adjacent to the Kentucky Fair and Exposition Center, we also had a contract to operate the fair's Midway and all of the games.

We had a mobile office and cash control room for the Midway. All those quarters that people throw into all those games add up, and there's a considerable amount of money that has to be taken in and out of each of the game operations and accounted for. Not only did we have this portable trailer; we also built a high security fence around it with a guard at the gate, thinking that was the best way to protect the money.

On the first night there was such a crowd—a mob scene, almost—on the Midway that a number of situations got out of hand: A few rowdy groups began to harass others, fights broke out, etc.

We were all on our walkie-talkies trying to control the situation. Meanwhile, the police were trying to corral all the trouble-makers.

Where did they establish their makeshift pen? Inside the fence surrounding the trailer with all the money. As I came down the Midway and saw this, I realized that more than half a million dollars in cash was enclosed in a fence that also was packed with about 118 thugs.

We quickly informed the police that a mere paper-thin wall separated these ne'er-do-wells from a big bunch of cash. Finally, we were able to secure the area.

Apparently, the rowdies never did know how close they came to being very rich rowdies.

A BRIDGE TOO FAR

Any amusement park developer knows that you situate the most interesting things at the back of the park, so that you'll draw people in, and they'll wind up seeing and doing everything in between. It's like placing the milk at the back of the grocery store.

Putting this philosophy to work was a tough assignment at the Royal Gorge Bridge, the world's highest suspension bridge, located in Canon City, Colorado.

Lupe Murchison hired LARC to improve and operate the bridge as a tourist attraction, which we did for eighteen years until she passed away.

We noticed that visitors would walk halfway across this bridge, be overwhelmed—you could put the Empire State Building underneath the bridge and the top of the building wouldn't touch the bridge—then look back to where their car was parked, get back in the car, and leave. We wanted them to stick around and spend some money.

So we had a plan that we would build a village across the bridge on the other side. We put up restaurants, crafts shops, theatres, etc. There was now a reason to go all the way across the bridge, to the far side.

We also built a berm (a small hill) so they couldn't see their cars.

Crafty, we were.

The visitors did indeed stay, and the more they stayed, the more they spent.

Royal Gorge became a tourist operation with truly gorgeous returns.

OH, DEER

We at LARC really do try to make people happy. Usually, it works. But Mother Nature has a weird sense of humor and sometimes likes to unravel our efforts just to see what will happen.

One of the first things Lupe Murchison always insisted on at the Royal Gorge Bridge, while we were running it, was heavy landscaping. No matter what we presented, she would always double the landscaping budget.

We finally learned, after several years of watching her spend shrubbery money that really wasn't necessary, to present only half of what was required. She'd promptly double the budget, and the result would be great landscaping.

We knew she loved red geraniums. So when she'd set a date to visit the attraction, I felt it would be appropriate to plant as many of them as we could at the bridge. So we planted geraniums in all the flower beds along the walkways and around the visitors center—wherever there was room to fit the flowers.

The afternoon before her visit, the area was a virtual Red Sea—just beautiful. Lovely red geraniums everywhere.

The next morning, I picked her up at the airport and drove to the bridge. I was horrified: There was not one geranium in sight. The deer had come in during the night and eaten all their heads off.

She took it well.

And I now know that geraniums make a good deer breakfast.

ALL'S WELL THAT ENDS WELL

You never know. A foreign visitor's first impression of America just might be you.

People living in gateway cities such as New York occasionally need to be reminded of that possibility. The choice is simple. Either you can be a gracious ambassador for your country or else you can morph into an "Ugly American."

I tried to be the former some years ago, but I'm afraid there was a U.S. Customs agent on hand equally determined to be the latter. I know these inspectors have a tough job, but this guy was way out of line.

The story began on a plane from Nigeria to New

York with two stops in Accra, Ghana, and Monrovia, Liberia, where we picked up passengers.

A whole family came on-board to send a young African boy to America. He was supposed to sit in a coach window seat next to me. I got up and let his mother sit next to him to say goodbye. It was a very tearful occasion, and I was touched to see the whole family on the plane to see him off. Obviously that couldn't happen today because of increased security.

Once the plane left the gate and began to taxi down the runway, I noticed the young man was sweating profusely. I showed him the air vent above him and later, when he took out a magazine, I showed him how to operate the light.

He seemed terribly grateful. It was obvious he'd never been on a plane before, but he spoke good English, and we soon fell into conversation. I learned that his entire family—father, mother, multiple sisters and brothers—had collected and sold aluminum cans for nine years to fund a trip to America for the young man. He had been accepted to study medicine at a school in South Carolina. The idea was that he'd return one day to Monrovia to practice medicine in his own country.

His emotions were so close to the surface. You could see how he was thrilled and scared at the same time. I'm not sure he slept at all during that long flight. All I know is that at 6:00 A.M. he punched me on the right shoulder to wake me up. He wanted to show me the Statue of Liberty as we flew over it. Well, I've seen the statue many times, of course. But, truth to tell, I've never seen it gleaming so beautifully as it caught the morning sun. This young man was so happy to be coming to America that his joy was positively infectious.

He made me feel like I was seeing the Statue of Liberty for the first time, too.

When the plane landed and the doors opened, and we walked from the airplane to the airport, he actually knelt down on the carpet and said aloud in an emotion-choked voice, "Thank God I've come to America!"

It was an unforgettable moment, followed almost immediately by one I wish I'd never witnessed. A customs agent pulled the young man aside and gave him a thoroughly rude going-over. I stayed behind and told the agent he didn't have to be so rough.

"This young man is just arriving in America to go to medical school here," I pleaded. The customs agent told me to get back across the line and to keep my mouth shut. Then I was motioned out of the area.

I felt so helpless and ashamed for my own country. I waited for my friend, and he came out looking quite the worse for his ordeal. He didn't seem to understand that he'd need to take a taxi from JFK where we'd landed to catch his next plane at LaGuardia: two different airports in the same city.

He was so shook up I just went ahead and took him in a taxi to LaGuardia, myself, and made sure that he caught his flight. I missed my own, but there's always another flight out of New York.

I stayed in touch with him while he was in med school and sent him a ticket to come to Dallas that Thanksgiving. Three months later a gift arrived from his parents in Monrovia. It was a rack of the horns of some animal, beautifully hand-carved and inscribed in poor English. His parents wrote that they didn't have anything to give, but here was a token they wanted me to have for helping their son. Those carved horns are still up in my office. They're so meaningful to me. It's not about what you have to give: it's about the spirit of giving.

The great part for me was being invited to the graduation ceremonies in South Carolina. I went there, feeling as though I was representing his family. I guess, at this point, we are family. He's now a physician in his native country, and we stay in touch to this day.

Afterword

Turnstiles continue to spin at the parks. Shows continue to open and perform. And, as I keep traveling, I continue to enjoy the people I meet and the places I go.

My past brought me to this point. The next generation—my son, Angus, who will continue to lead LARC; my daughter, Delanie, a professor and well-known artist; and my daughter, Tiffany, a marine biologist and librarian—will continue to entertain in their own distinct careers, and I look forward to reading their stories. My granddaughter, Lila Grace—who knows the stories she will see and experience in her lifetime?

I am thankful to Angus G. Wynne, Jr. and Luther D. Clark for the great opportunities they gave me in my early career. Also, to John M. Stemmons and Trammell Crow for the vision and mentoring they provided.

Finally, I would like to thank the officers and Board of Directors of Dallas Summer Musicals, who have given me the opportunity to continue to experience such an unusual career.

Michael teams up with the Rockettes.

Show Business is two words: it's about being creative and putting on the *show*, but just as important is running it like a *business*.

Michael and Wendy Jenkins with Jay Leno.

Michael is friendly to everyone, including Casper.

Granddaughter Lila Grace and Michael.

Awards

2003
Dallas Historical Society Award for Excellence
in Community Service for Outstanding
Contributions in Arts Leadership

2003
First Baptist Church of Dallas Sanctuary Choir
Honorary Member

2003
Dallas Theatre League Nomination for
Leon Rabin Award for Outstanding Achievement
in the Production of a Musical—
Thoroughly Modern Millie

2002
Dallas Theatre League Nomination for
Leon Rabin Award for Outstanding Achievement
in the Production of a Musical—*Some Like It Hot*

2002
School of Music, Yale University,
Cultural Leadership Citation—
Recognition of Service to the
Cultural Life of a Nation

2002
International Association of Amusement Parks and
Attractions Brass Ring Award for Marketing

2000
Spirit of Centennial Award for Long-standing
Commitment and Service to Fair Park

1997
Dallas Theatre League Nomination for Leon Rabin
Award for Outstanding Achievement in the
Production of a Musical—*The King & I*

Five-time recipient of IAAPA recognition
for outstanding contributions
to the amusement industry

Bureau of International Fairs and World Expositions
Award for Best Entertainment Zone Developed,
The 1982 World's Fair

Texas Showman's Association Entrepreneur Award

Associations

AIMS International
American Heart Association–Dallas Division
   (Immediate Past Chair)
American Institute of Architects
Dallas County Heritage Society (Board of Directors)
Independent Presenter's Network
International Association of Amusement Parks and
   Attractions (IAAPA)
International Association of Assembly Managers
International Association of Fairs and Expositions
International Association of Family Entertainment
   Centers
International Council of Shopping Centers
The League of American Theatres and Producers
Leon Rabin Awards
National Alliance for Musical Theatre (President)
Nationwide Financial Solutions (Board of Directors)
Outdoor Amusement Business Association
Producers Four (Producer)
RG America (Board of Directors)
Southeast Tourism Society
Themed Entertainment Association
Tony Awards Voter
Troika Entertainment (Board of Directors)
Urban Land Institute

Variety Club of North Texas (Board of Directors)
World Waterpark Association

PREVIOUSLY HELD
BOARD OF DIRECTOR POSITIONS

Alfa SmartParks
Dallas Theatre Center
Harlem Globetrotters
Ice Capades
International Association of Amusement Parks and
    Attractions (IAAPA)
International Broadcasting Corporation
Shakespeare Festival of Dallas
Silverleaf Resorts
State Fair of Texas President's Task Force

Broadway and National Tours

ON-BROADWAY

A Day in Hollywood / A Night in the Ukraine
Big River
Bombay Dreams
Brooklyn
Fascinating Rhythm
The 5,000 Fingers of Dr. T (in production for 2006)
Flower Drum Song
Gem of the Ocean
High Society
I Remember Mama
King Hedley II
The King and I
Sixteen Wounded
Thoroughly Modern Millie

OFF-BROADWAY

I Got Merman
Summer of '42
Thunder Knocking On the Door

NATIONAL TOURS

Annie Get Your Gun

Big River
Copacabana
Flower Drum Song
Jose Greco and Spanish Dancers
Joseph and the Amazing Technicolor Dreamcoat
The King and I
The Music Man
My Fair Lady
Oklahoma!
On a Clear Day You Can See Forever
Smokey Joe's Café
Some Like It Hot
South Pacific
Stop the World, I Want to Get Off
Thoroughly Modern Millie
Will Rogers Follies
The Wizard of Oz

OTHER PRODUCTIONS

CBS National Telecast of Miss Teenage America
    Pageant (four years)
Crystal Charity Ball–Cirque de Noël–1993
Dr. Pepper Annual Bottlers Meeting
Heartland
The Incredible Acrobats of China
University of North Texas Centennial Celebration
    Extravaganza–1990
Yale University Tercentennial Extravaganza–2001

In addition to more than eighty productions produced
for Six Flags Over Texas, Six Flags Over Georgia, Baylor
University, First Baptist Church of Dallas, various cor-
porations and industrial shows.

Musicals Produced and/or Presented in Dallas, Texas

Music Hall at Fair Park and The Majestic Theatre
Dallas Summer Musicals and Broadway Contemporary Series

1995

1. *Sisters Rosenweig*
2. *Hello Dolly*
3. *Grease*
4. *Stage Door Charley*
5. *Cinderella*
6. *Singin' in the Rain*
7. *Joseph and the Amazing Technicolor Dreamcoat*
8. *Crazy for You*
9. *Jekyll and Hyde*
10. *The Phantom of the Opera*
11. *A Tuna Christmas*
12. *Laughter on the 23rd Floor*
13. *Mannheim Steamroller*

1996

14. *An Inspector Calls*
15. *Ain't Misbehavin'*

16. *Grease*
17. *Kiss of the Spider Woman*
18. *Carousel*
19. *Damn Yankees*
20. *Music of the Night*
21. *West Side Story*
22. *How to Succeed in Business without Really Trying*
23. *Miss Saigon*
24. *Deathtrap*

1997

25. *Master Class*
26. *Man of La Mancha*
27. *A Chorus Line*
28. *Smokey Joe's Café*
29. *The Music Man*
30. *The King and I*
31. *Les Misérables*
32. *Cats*
33. *Cirque Ingenieux*
34. *Beauty and the Beast*
35. *Tap Dogs*
36. *A Tuna Christmas*
37. *Rent*

1998

38. *National Ballet of Spain*
39. *Chicago*
40. *David Copperfield*
41. *Annie*
42. *Joseph and the Amazing Technicolor Dreamcoat*
43. *Oklahoma!*
44. *Big*
45. *Porgy and Bess*—Miles Davis/Gershwins

46. *Peter Pan*
47. *Bring in Da Noise/Bring in Da Funk*
48. *Riverdance*
49. *Show Boat*
50. *Grease*
51. *The Gin Game*

1999
52. *Moon Over Buffalo*
53. *Red, White and Tuna*
54. *Victor Victoria*
55. *Evita*
56. *Blind Lemon*
57. *Jekyll and Hyde*
58. *Cirque Ingenieux*
59. *South Pacific*
60. *Footloose*
61. *Sunset Blvd.*
62. *The Scarlet Pimpernel*
63. *Jolson*
64. *Ragtime*
65. *Titanic*
66. *South Pacific*—Pasadena, California
67. *Jolson*—Pasadena, California
68. *Joseph and the Amazing Technicolor Dreamcoat*
69. *A Celebration of the Classic Hollywood Musicals*
70. *Rent*
71. *Art*
72. *A Tuna Christmas*

2000
73. *The Male Intellect: An Oxymoron?*
74. *Tony N' Tina's Wedding*
75. *Fame*

76. *Selena*
77. *Cabaret*
78. *Fosse*
79. *The Sound of Music*
80. *Parade*
81. *Riverdance*
82. *Annie Get Your Gun*
83. *Copacabana*—Toronto
84. *Smokey Joe's Café*
85. *The Music of Andrew Lloyd Webber*
86. *The Phantom of the Opera*
87. *Smokey Joe's Café*—Pasadena, California
88. *The Music of Andrew Lloyd Webber*—Pasadena, California
89. *Copacabana*
90. *Fame*—Pasadena, California
91. *Chicago*

2001
92. *Tallulah*
93. *Lido–La Tournée*
94. *Jekyll and Hyde*
95. *Copperfield*
96. *Fiddler on the Roof*
97. *Forever Plaid*
98. *Blue's Clues Live!*
99. *Arthur, a Live Adventure*
100. *Leader of the Pack*
101. *The Best Little Whorehouse in Texas*
102. *The Civil War*
103. *Les Misérables*
104. *Cinderella*
105. *Dame Edna*

106. *Casper*
107. *Kiss Me, Kate*
108. *Saturday Night Fever*
109. *Aida*
110. *Les Misérables*—Pasadena, California
111. *Tap Dogs*

2002

112. *Red, White and Tuna*
113. *Always Patsy Cline*
114. *A Tuna Christmas*
115. *Dirty Blonde*
116. *Proof*
117. *Swing!*
118. *Cats*
119. *Contact*
120. *The Wizard of Oz*
121. *Blast*
122. *Some Like It Hot*
123. *Stomp*
124. *My Fair Lady*
125. *42nd Street*
126. *The Lion King*
127. *Radio City Christmas Spectacular*

2003

128. *Tick Tick Boom*
129. *Burn the Floor*
130. *Dora the Explorer*
131. *Seussical*
132. *Blast*
133. *Cirque Dream It Live*
134. *Beauty and the Beast*
135. *Will Rogers Follies*

136. *Thoroughly Modern Millie*
137. *Starlight Express*
138. *Flower Drum Song*
139. *Mamma Mia!*
140. *I Got Merman*
141. *A Tuna Christmas*
142. *A Night with Dame Edna*

2004
143. *Say Goodnight Gracie*
144. *Heartland*
145. *Def Poetry Jam*
146. *Chicago*
147. *Copperfield*
148. *Nunsense*
149. *Seinfeld*
150. *Bill Cosby*
151. *Miss Saigon*
152. *Lord of the Dance*
153. *Yankee Doodle Dandy*
154. *The King and I*
155. *Big River*
156. *Little Shop of Horrors*
157. *Tap Dogs*
158. *Joseph and the Amazing Technicolor Dreamcoat*
159. *Jesus Christ Superstar*
160. *The Graduate*
161. *Fosse*
162. *Cinderella on Ice*

2005
163. *Oklahoma!*
164. *The Ten Tenors*

165. *Cookin'*
166. *Hairspray*
167. *Peter Pan*
168. *The Producers*
169. *On the Record*
170. *Movin' Out*
171. *Dr. Dolittle*
172. *Wicked*

LARC Project List

AUSTRALIA
Dreamworld, Coomera
Isle of Capri, Gold Coast
Casino, Gold Coast
Cades County Water Park, Gold Coast
Jennings Industries, Gold Coast
Fantasy World/Fisherman's Wharf, Gold Coast
Paradise Center, Gold Coast
Santa Barbara Water Wonderland, Gold Coast
Fun City, Gold Coast
Koala Park, Sydney
Luna Park, Sydney
Darling Walk/Darling Harbour, Sydney
Pier One, Sydney
Family Fun Park, Sydney
Tilt/Manly Indoor Entertainment, Sydney
Manly Pier, Sydney
O'Neill's Great Adventure, Sydney
The Story of Sydney, Sydney
Water Park, Melbourne
Werribee Park, Melbourne
Capital Bakery, Melbourne
Western Gardens, Melbourne

Holdfast Shores Themed Entertainment Complex,
 Adelaide
Splashville, Adelaide
Recreation Center, Penrith, New South Wales
Magic Mountain, Nobby Beach, Queensland
Aqua World, Bribie Island
Bartlett's Water Park, Nerang
Jindalee Water Park, Brisbane
Expo '88, Brisbane
Splashville, Darwin
Splashville, Perth
Water Wonderland, Campbelltown
Water Wonderland, Warriewood
Water World, Underwood
Greater Union Theater, Mermaid Beach
Hoyt's Theatres
The Brick Works, Canberra
Canberra Fair Village
Royal Easter Show, Crossroads

BAHAMAS
Luna Park, Nassau
Aqua World, Nassau
Alexander's World Resort, Exuma

BAHRAIN
Pearl Island

BRAZIL
Neptune's Kingdom, Cabo Frio
Parque Sauipe, Salvador, Bahia
Sao Paulo Theme Park, Sao Paulo
Barra Shopping Center, Sao Paulo

CANADA

Harbourfront, Ontario
Ontario Place, Ontario
Prudhomme Project, Ontario
Lansdowne Park, Ottawa
Toronto's World Fair, Toronto
Claireville Water Park, Toronto
Oceanic Adventures Aquarium, Toronto
Toronto Water Way 401, Toronto
Interactive Entertainment Center, Toronto
Laval Themed Entertainment Center, Quebec
Aquarium Industry, Montreal, Quebec
Nova Scotia Tourism Family Entertainment Center,
    Nova Scotia
Magic Valley, Nova Scotia
Gravity House, Bedford, Nova Scotia
Heritage Village, Nova Scotia
Alberta Oil Museum, Leduc, Alberta
Atlas Coal Mine, Edmonton
Dinosaur Copper Cove, Edmonton
Fort Edmonton, Edmonton, Alberta
Edmonton Space and Science Center, Edmonton,
    Alberta
Empress Industries, Vancouver,
    British Columbia
Wasaga Beach II, Wasaga Beach

CHINA

Dragon Lake Park, Shantou
Mini-Golf, Guangzhou

COLUMBIA

Theme Park, Bogota

CYPRUS
Cyprus Family Entertainment Center, Limassol

DENMARK
Farup Theme Park
Lego World, Billund

ECUADOR
Family Entertainment Center, Quito

EGYPT
Theme Park, Cairo

FRANCE
Parc du Vivant Health Pavilion, Lille
Paris Parc, Paris
Zygofolis, Nice

GERMANY
Aeroworld, Frankfurt
African Village, Hamburg

GREECE
Corfu Waterpark, Corfu

INDIA
Bangalore Theme Park, Bangalore
Madras Theme Park, Madras

INDONESIA
Awani Leisure Park, Jakarta
Kelapa Gading Mega Mall, Jakarta

Cariu Leisure Park
Parangtritis Leisure Park
Trawas Leisure Park

IRELAND
Boyne Park of National Heritage
Laganside, Belfast

ITALY
Rimini Theme Park, Rimini
Aquafan Water Park, Rimini
Fasano Water Park, Fasano
Killer Whales, Sciaccamare
Rome Waterpark, Rome
Tagliacozzo Waterpark, Tagliacozzo
Versilia Water Park/Retail, Versilia
Venice Theme Park, Venice

JAPAN
Todeco, Tokyo
SOGO Department Store, Tokyo
Tokyo Amphitheater, Tokyo
National Football League Luxury Suites
    and Penthouses, Tokyo
Toppan, Tokyo
Health Pavilion, Nagoya

KOREA
Seoul Land, Seoul

KUWAIT
Theme Park Expansion, Safat
Future Kid Arcade, Safat

Messilla Beach Water Village

MALAYSIA
Bukit Tinggi Theme Park, Kuala Lumpur
SamaWorld, Kuala Lumpur
Themed Attraction, Melaka

MEXICO
Themed Entertainment Center,
    Nuevo Laredo
Parque La Pastora, Nuevo Leon
Themed Attraction, Cabo San Lucas
Water Park, Puebla
Queretary Park, Queretaro
Mundo Deadeveras Children's Interactive Museum,
    Monterrey
Proyecto Alegria, Monterrey
Restaurant/Entertainment/Retail, Acapulco
Parque Nizuc Water Park, Cancun

NEW ZEALAND
Leisure Park Club, Auckland
Rainbow's End, Auckland
John Reid's Squash Center, Auckland
Auckland Water Park, Auckland
Water Theme Park, Christchurch

PHILIPPINES
Robinson's Galleria Family Entertainment Center,
    Manila

NIGERIA
Apapa Park/Ikoyi Park, Lagos

LAVAM Child Care and Family Entertainment Center,
    Owerri, Imo
Nigerian Trade Fair
Heritage City, Abuja

NORWAY
TusenFryd, Oslo

PHILIPPINES
Themed Attraction, Manila
Robinson's Commercial Complex, Ermita, Manila

PUERTO RICO
Theme Park/Resort Development, Aguadilla

RUSSIA
Magic Land Theme Park, Sochi

SAUDI ARABIA
Amusement Tent Park, Riyadh
Dammam Amusement Park, Dammam
Gulf Amusement Park, Riyadh
Star City, Riyadh
Mega Theme Park, Jeddah

SICILY
Tourist Village Primosole, Cantina

SINGAPORE
Fun Station/Fantasy Island
Entertainment Mall/Fantasy Island
Kings Center

Orchard Hotel Interiors
Imagine
Fantasy Island, Sentosa Island

SPAIN
Disneyland Development
Theme Park, Seville
Seven Palms Entertainment Complex, Las Palmas
Expo '92, Seville
Aqua Madrid Waterpark, Madrid

THAILAND
Siam Park, Bangkok
Water Theme Park, Pattaya

UNITED ARAB EMIRATES
Falcon View Park, Abu Dhabi
WonderLand Theme Park, Dubai
Water Mist Show, Dubai
WonderLand Water Park, Dubai

UNITED KINGDOM
Alton Towers, North Staffordshire
Trentham Gardens, North Staffordshire
American Adventure Theme Park, Derbyshire
Battersea Power Station, London
Maritime Museum, London
Thomas the Tank Engine, England
Breco, Seven Oaks, Kent
Carden Park, Chester
Poddington Peas, Essex
Milton Keynes Miniature Golf Course
Brooklands Museum, Weybridge

VENEZUELA
Magic Park, Caracas
Ride Procurement, Caracas
Family Entertainment Facility, Caracas
Themed Amusement Park, Maracaibo
Lago Encantado, Maracay
Pampatar Water Park, Isla Margarita
Isla Bella Theme Park, Margarita

WEST AFRICA
Ghana Family Entertainment Area, Ghana

UNITED STATES
Alabama
Canyonland, Leesburg
Mobile Theme Park, Mobile
Nocalusa Falls, Gadsden

Arizona
Walnut Canyon Gateway Railroad Attraction,
    Flagstaff
Rawhide Western Theme Park at Fort McDowell
    Yavapai Nation, Fountain Hills
Coors Grand Canyon Showcase, Grand Canyon
Village of Monte Vista, Mesa
Phoenix Music Park, Phoenix
Phoenix Theme Park, Phoenix
Medical Expo, Phoenix
Ragin' River, Phoenix
Rawhide, Scottsdale
Oceanic Adventures Aquarium, Scottsdale
Old Tucson Play Area, Tucson
Arizona Territory, Williams

Arkansas
Dogpatch U.S.A., Harrison
Daryl Lusby Motorplex, Pine Bluff
Eureka Springs Theme Park, Eureka Springs
The Great Passion Play, Eureka Springs
America's Christmas Village, Eureka Springs
Wax Works, Eureka Springs
Miracles Theater Building for The Great Passion Play,
    Eureka Springs
Re-Development of The Great Passion Play, Eureka
    Springs
Eureka Springs Tourism Development, Eureka Springs
Mount Air Lodge, Eureka Springs
Eureka Springs Railroad, Eureka Springs
Magic Springs, Hot Springs
Ogden Food Building Magic Springs, Hot Springs
Hope Tourist Train, Hope
Ozark Mountain Railroad, Oak Grove
Fun City, Lake of the Ozarks
Ozark Folk Center, Mountain View
War Memorial Park, Little Rock
Bella Vista Village, Bella Vista Village

California
Anaheim Kiddie Park, Anaheim
Walt Disney Productions-Consulting, Burbank
Lion Country Safari, Laguna Hills
Micki Grove Park, Lodi
Proposed Theme Park, Auburn
Entertainment Center at Moreno Valley Mall, Moreno
Castle Park, Riverside
Family Entertainment Center and Skate Center, Riverside
In-Line Hockey Family Entertainment Center, San Diego

Sidewalk Surfparks, San Diego
Champagne Gardens Botanical Gardens,
    San Diego
Pier 39 Aquarium, San Francisco
Nut Tree Development, Vacaville
Tilt (Valico), Cupertino
Club Kokomo, Los Angeles
Old Towne, Los Angeles
Soft Ball Diamond, Los Angeles
Hooray for Hollywood, Hollywood
Aqua Thrill, Livermore
Kathryn Hall Vineyards Tasting Room, Napa
Poway Water Park, Poway
Raging Waters, San Dimas
Western Water World, Bakersfield

Colorado
Motor World, Colorado Springs
Seven Falls, Colorado Springs
Royal Gorge Bridge and Park, Canon City
Research for Entertainment Industry, Denver
Cinderella City Mall, Englewood
Colorado's West World, Erie Junction
Pine Lakes Village, Denver
Ice Skating Rink, Denver
Rio Grande Railroad, Denver
Celebrity Sports Center, Denver
Castle Rock Water Park, Denver
Forum Fair, Durango
Forum Fair, Glenwood Springs
Riverfront Festival Center, Littleton
Colorado West World, Loveland
Water Park, Lakewood

Connecticut
Lake Compounce, Bristol
Yale University Tercentennial Celebration, New Haven

Florida
Action Park, Jacksonville
Adventure Park, Jacksonville
Sally Industries, Jacksonville
Shabu-Shabu, Jacksonville
Forum Fair, Regency Square, Jacksonville
Market Assessment Analysis for Alfa SmartParks,
    Jacksonville
Busch Gardens, Tampa
Interama, Miami Lakes
Marco Polo, Daytona Beach
Miracle Strip Amusement Park, Panama City
Southern Amusements, West Palm Beach
Aquatic Complex, West Palm Beach
St. Lucie Theme Park, St. Lucie
Treasure Island, Miami
Tropical Wonderland, Titusville
Indoor Entertainment Center, Margate
Sports Complex, Naples
Little England, Orlando
Hemispheres Project, Orlando
Horseworld (Park Equis), Orlando
Venetian Glass Pavilion, Orlando
James E. Strates Shows, Orlando
Orlando Theme Park, Orlando
Paradise Park, Orlando
Western Fun World, Orlando
Land Development, Orlando
Kapok Tree Inns, Clearwater

Weeki Wachie, Weeki Wachie Springs
Camping World, Kissimmee
Seminole Tribe of Florida, Hollywood
Long Beach Resort, Panama City
Shipwreck Island, Panama City
Fort Lauderdale Water Park, Ft. Lauderdale
Water World, Ft. Lauderdale
Crystal Palace, Ft. Lauderdale
Emmett Kelley Circus, Ft. Lauderdale
Tallahassee Water Theme Park, Tallahassee
Wild Waters, Silver Springs
Silver Springs Nature Park, Silver Springs

Georgia
Alice's Wonderland, Albany
Kingdom's Three, Atlanta
Agricultural Exposition Center, Atlanta
Atlanta Aquarium, Atlanta
Georgia Heritage Special Train, Atlanta
Omni Fair, Atlanta
Atlanta Olympic Street Festival, Atlanta
Six Flags Over Georgia, Atlanta
Folkways Center, Dahlonega
Lookout Mountain Themed Attraction, Lookout Mountain
Rock City Gardens, Lookout Mountain
Savannah Theme Park, Savannah
Fowler Wildlife, Savannah
Savannah Quarters, Savannah
Georgia Golf Hall of Fame, Augusta
Georgia Agricultural Business Center, Bulloch County
In Clover Concerts, Pelham
Clayton County Amphitheater, Jonesboro
Gone With the Wind, Clayton County, Jonesboro

Dunaway Gardens, Newnan
Jim Fowler Life in the Wild, Brunswick
Cabbage Patch Babyland Village and Art School, Cleveland
Northeastern Georgia Regional Tourism Development

Hawaii
Aloha Park, Honolulu
Film/Video Production Industry, Honolulu
Blackfield Hawaii, Honolulu
Fun Factory, Honolulu
Kahuku Sugar Mill, Honolulu
Oahu Feasibility Study and Master Plan, Oahu
Amfac-Part II (Horizons), Oahu
Hawaiian Sea Village, Maui

Illinois
Old Chicago, Bolingbrook
Village of Rosemont, Rosemont
Aladdin's Castle, Chicago
Bally Manufacturing Corporation, Chicago
Chicago Bears, Chicago
International Amphitheater, Chicago
Here's Chicago, Chicago
IAAPA, Chicago
Magic Waters, Rockford
Pekin Water Park, Pekin
R.S. Wallace Power Station, Peoria

Indiana
Fair Oaks Dairy Farm Adventure, Fair Oaks
Historical Amusement Foundation, Indianapolis
Riley Village, Indianapolis
Wicker Park, Highland

Water Theme Park

Iowa
Adventureland Park, Des Moines
Earthdom Study, Davenport

Kansas
Emerald City/Land of Oz, Lenexa
Theme Park, Wichita
Towne West Square, Wichita
Martha's Pizza Stix, Shawnee Mission

Kentucky
Beech Bend Park, Bowling Green
Camping World, Bowling Green
Christmas Park, Cave City
Cave City Convention and Civic Center, Cave City
Mammoth Cave Park, Cave City
Kentucky Kingdom, Louisville
Music Fest, Louisville
Kentucky Fair and Exposition Center, Louisville
Louisville Pizza Stix, Louisville
Entertainment Facility, Paducah
Cumberland Falls, Corbin
Newport Aquarium, Newport

Louisiana
Amusement Attractions, Baton Rouge
Catfish House, Baton Rouge
Mixed-Use Recreation Project, Baton Rouge
Cajun World, New Orleans
Airline Highway, New Orleans
Jazzland Water Park, New Orleans

Multi-Use Leisure Attraction, New Orleans
New Orleans Amphitheater, New Orleans
Civic Theatre, New Orleans
New Orleans Highway Project, New Orleans
Jazzland, New Orleans
Lake Forest Plaza, New Orleans
Delta Village, Tallulah
Hamel's Park, Shreveport
Hamel's Zoo Park, Shreveport
Water Town, Shreveport
Penny Whistle Park, Shreveport
Louisiana Downs, Shreveport
Family Entertainment Center, Covington
Global Golf Academy, Lafayette
Mixed-Use Recreation Project, Lafayette
Caldwell Parish Mixed-Use Development, Columbia

Maine
Ocean Spray, Lakeville
Old Orchard Beach, Old Orchard Beach

Maryland
Playland Park, Ocean City
RTKL Associates, Baltimore
Unique Design, Finksburg

Massachusetts
Midway Park, Salisbury
Splash and Dash, Newburyport
Water Park Recreation Center, Worcester
Paragon Park, Hull
Hall Estate Family Entertainment Center, Hull
Cranberry World, Plymouth

Maritime Museum, Plymouth
Edaville Railroad, South Carver

Michigan
Antique Village, Clarkston
Auto World, Flint
Boblo Island, Detroit
Little Michigan, Detroit
Boblo Island Games, Detroit
Kinitex, Detroit
S&H Vending, Detroit
Indian World, Mackinac Highlands
Jones Is Back, Jones
St. Ignace Attraction, St. Ignace
Theme Park, Iron Mountain
Antique Village, Lake Orion
Grand River Technologies, Grand River
Water Park, Monroe

Minnesota
Valleyfair, Shakopee
General Mills Entertainment Center, Minneapolis
Expansion and Redevelopment of a Mixed-Use Project,
    Monticello
Osowski's Orchard, Monticello
Aquarium/Mall of America, Bloomington

Mississippi
America's Park, Gulfport
Themed Attraction, Gulfport
Trinity Ranch, Gulfport
Olympus Water Park, Gulfport
Dixieland USA, Jackson

Farrow Amusements, Jackson
Theme Park, Richland/Jackson
Theme Park, Vancleave

Missouri
Branson Theme Park, Branson
Entertainment Project, Branson
Rockaway Beach, Branson
Branson Live!, Branson
Six Flags Over Mid-America, Eureka
Ozark Fun City, Springfield
Fort of the Osage, Osage Beach
Themed Attraction, St. Joseph
Truman Lake, Warsaw
Midway Golf, Kansas City
Midway Mall, Kansas City
Lake of the Ozarks Attraction,
    Lake of the Ozarks
Fort of the Ozarks, Lake of the Ozarks
Tilt - Northwest Plaza, St. Ann
Missouri State Fair, Sedalia

Nebraska
Peony Park, Omaha

Nevada
Old Vegas, Henderson
Theme Park, Wendover
Old Vegas Train Restoration, Henderson
America in Miniature, Las Vegas
South Star, Las Vegas
Wet 'n Wild, Las Vegas
Fun Factory, Las Vegas

Las Vegas Aquarium, Las Vegas
Chameleon Technologies, Las Vegas

New Hampshire
Benson's Animal Farm, Hudson
Santa's Village, Jefferson

New Jersey
Indoor Family Entertainment Center, Cherry Hill
Crystal Palace, Edgewater
Great Adventure, Jackson
King Two Koncepts, Maple Shade
Land of Make Believe, Hope
Morey's Pier, Wildwood
Ramagosa Projects, Sportland Pier, North Wildwood
Wild West City, Netcong
Asbury Casino Entertainment Center, Asbury Park
Atlantic City Family Entertainment Center, Atlantic City
Liberty Park Casino, Pier and Pool, Seaside Heights
Royal Arcade, Seaside Heights
Proposed Family Entertainment Center, Wayne
Themed Entertainment Facility, Scotch Plains
Tilt at Echelon Mall, Voorhees
Sacony Industries, Trenton Falls
Union MarketPlace, Vauxhall Union
Hunt Circus, Florence

New Mexico
Albuquerque Themed Attraction, Albuquerque
Uncle Cliff's Park, Albuquerque
Desert Ocean, Albuquerque
Ruidoso Park, Ruidoso
Lincoln County Theatre, Ruidoso

Sierra Sinema, Ruidoso
Roswell Rapids, Roswell

New York
Action Park, Lake George
The Great Escape, Lake George
Rainbow International Garden, Lake George
Adventurers Park, Long Island
Buccaneer Theme Park, Huntington, Long Island
Carnival Amusements, Copiague
Coney Island, Coney Island
Steeplechase Park, Coney Island
Crystal Palace, Brooklyn
NBC Theme Park Industry Analysis, New York City
Pier 63, New York
Roseland Park, Canandaigua
Ed MacMahon Fun Palace, Wildwood
Festival Marketplace, Batavia
Statue of Liberty, Ellis Island
Lake Placid Resort, Lake Placid
Doron Precision Simulators, Binghamton
Staten Island/Garden State/Mt. Olive, Palisades
The Great Escape (Tahitian Tempest), Glen Falls

North Carolina
Charlotte Theme Park, Charlotte
Heritage USA, Charlotte
Forge Valley Park, Horseshoe
The Alpert Corporation, Greensboro
Theme Park, Raleigh
Cabarrus County Exhibition Park, Concord
Concord Exhibition Park, Concord
Tad's Landing Mixed-Use Development, Rowland

Eastern North Carolina Tourism Development
Cherokee Magic Waters, Maggie Valley
Emerald Pointe, Winston/Salem

Ohio
Idora Park, Youngstown
United Skates of America, Columbus
Gooding Zoo Park, Powell
Advertising Presentation to Cedar Point,
    Fairlawn
Montgomery County Wave Pool, Dayton

Oklahoma
Discoveryland, Tulsa
River City, Tulsa
Wild Waters, Tulsa
Bell's Surf and Slide, Tulsa
Old Testament Scenes Exhibit, Tulsa
Casa Bonita, Tulsa
Park Lane Shopping Center, Tulsa
Fort Gibson, Tulsa
Frontier City USA, Oklahoma City
Muscogee (Creek) Indian Nation, Sapulpa
Theme Park, Henryetta
Theme Park, Muskogee
Dillingham Ranch, Okmulgee
Crafters Marketplace Environmental Restaurant,
    Oklahoma City
Arbuckle Wilderness, Davis
Guest Ranch, Durant
Grand Lake Association, Grove
Oceanside Oklahoma, Norman

Oregon
The Oaks Amusement Park, Portland
Time Traveler Park, Salem
Blue Lake Family Center, Multnomah County
Cove Canyon Enterprises, Madras

Pennsylvania
Dorney Park, Allentown
Dorney Park's Wild Water Kingdom, Allentown
Hersheypark, Hershey
Old Towne Concept, Hershey
Kennywood Park, West Mifflin
Penn's Landing, Philadelphia
National Constitution Center, Philadelphia
Pocono's Magic Valley, Bushkill
Point Development Leisure Park, Clarion
Diamond Peak Family Fun Center, New Brighton
International Golf and Recreation Family
    Entertainment Center, Scranton
Cowboy Truckstop, Milesburg
International Palace of Food and Fun, Bristol

South Carolina
Bowling Alley, Hilton Head Island
Family Theme Park, Myrtle Beach
Pavilion Amusement Park, Myrtle Beach
Themed Attraction, North Myrtle Beach
NASCAR Themed Amusement Area,
    Myrtle Beach
A.R.E.A. Seminar, Greenville

South Dakota
City of Deadwood, Deadwood

Tennessee
Chilhowie Park, Knoxville
1982 World's Fair, Knoxville
World Class Food and Beverage, Knoxville
Cruisin' USA, Nashville
Twitty City, Nashville
Opryland, Nashville
Fifty States, Gatlinburg
Smoky Mountain Farms, Gatlinburg
Christus Gardens, Gatlinburg
Graceland, Memphis
Libertyland, Memphis
Lake Winnepesaukah, Chattanooga
Moccasin Bend, Chattanooga
Silver Dollar City, Pigeon Forge
Water Circus, Pigeon Forge
The Universe, Sevierville

Texas
Paradise Park of Abilene, Abilene
Texas Forts Trail Visitor Center and Transportation
    Museum, Abilene
Frontier Texas!, Abilene
Rainy Creek, Abilene
Exasco, Alvarado
Arlington Convention and Visitors Bureau, Arlington
Empire Park, Arlington
Forum Fair, Arlington
Gold Coast, Arlington
Lion Country Safari, Arlington
Six Flags Over Texas, Arlington
Sportorama, Six Flags Mall, Arlington
The Way, Arlington

Town and Country Cleaners, Arlington
Wet 'n Wild, Arlington
Austin Theme Park, Austin
Austin Water Park, Austin
Cherry Springs Ranch, Austin
Texas Independence Express, Austin
Water Space Park, Austin
Wild Blue Yonder Airplane Museum, Austin
Adventure Kingdom, Beaumont
Beaumont Convention and Visitors Bureau, Beaumont
Houseman Recreation Project, Beaumont
Water Park, Beaumont
Resort, Big Springs
Amigoland, Brownsville
Fun Time Pizza, Carrollton
Family Entertainment Center, Clear Lake
Moore's Driving Range, Colleyville
Grapevine Springs, Coppell
Theme Park, Copperas Cove
Texas Riviera, Corpus Christi
Aladdin's Castle at Red Bird Mall, Dallas
Nickels and Dimes, Dallas
Oil Supply Building, West End, Dallas
Penny Whistle Park, Dallas
Shopping Center Themed Attraction, Dallas
Scotty's Golf Park, Dallas
Shake, Rattle and Roll, Dallas
West End Amusements, Dallas
Audio Visual, Red Bird Mall, Dallas
West End Cowboy Shop, Dallas
Dallas Fire Museum, Dallas
Military Museum, Dallas
Peter Wolf Associates, Dallas

Wax World, Dallas
Cinnamon Junction, Dallas
Texas Long Bar, West End, Dallas
Hank's Chuck Wagon, Dallas
Magic Castle Restaurant, Dallas
IMAX, Dallas
Loews Anatole, Dallas
Texas Theater Renovation, Dallas
The Design Experience, Dallas
What's New Theatre Project IT, IAAPA, Dallas
Dynapark, Dallas
Fun Corporation of America, Dallas
Garnet Walker Games Building, Dallas
Crystal Charity Ball, Dallas
Shakespeare Festival of Dallas, Dallas
State Fair of Texas, Dallas
Super Show, Dallas
TACA Ball 1997, Dallas
The Incredible Acrobats of China, Dallas
Big D Ranch, Dallas
City Place Project, Dallas
Blackland Properties, Dallas
Farm Village, Dallas
Texas Industries, Dallas
Peter Piper Pizza, El Paso
Scotty's Sports Park, Euless
Dinosaur Exhibit, Fort Worth Museum of Science and
    History, Fort Worth
Fort Worth Museum of Science and History Expansion,
    Fort Worth
Cowboys and Indians Fort Worth Stockyard, Fort Worth
Indoor Entertainment Center - Town Center Mall, Fort
    Worth

Trinity Park Center, Fort Worth
Westridge Mall, Fort Worth
Frank Buck Zoo, Gainesville
Gainesville Events Center, Gainesville
Gainesville Airport Park, Gainesville
Leonard Park, Gainesville
Strategic Tourism Development, Gainesville
Galveston County Parks, Galveston
Moody Foundation, Galveston
Inner Space Cavern, Georgetown
Worthy is the Lamb, Glen Rose
Boardwalk Family Fun Park, Grand Prairie
Native American Heritage Museum, Grapevine
Opry House, Grapevine
Tourism Study, Harlingen
Plaza de Toros, Houston
Putt-Putt Golf Course, Houston
Galleria, Houston
Parkshire Shopping Center, Houston
Albert Thomas Convention Center, Houston
Danbury Park, Houston
Fame City, Houston
Family Fun Fair, Houston
Water Park, Houston
HEB Indoor Park, Hurst/Euless/Bedford
Texas Stadium Pavilion, Irving
Marketplace Carousel, Irving
Cowboys ShowPlace, Irving
Las Colinas Movie Studio Tour, Irving
Valley Ranch Floodplain, Irving
Splash Down Water Park, Irving
The Living Waters Passion Play, Johnson City
Dude Ranch, Justin

LaGrange Waterpark, LaGrange
La Bota Ranch, Laredo
La Placita Village, Laredo
Laredo Park, Laredo
Nuevo Laredo, Nuevo Laredo
Quinta Mazatlan Nature Center, McAllen
Yesteryear, Madisonville
Mixed-Use Entertainment Development, Mesquite
Heart of Texas Theme Park, New Braunfels
Beer Garden, Odessa
Ector County Coliseum and Exhibition Center, Odessa
Water Wonderland, Odessa
Crawgator Water Park, Orange
LMCI Acquisition Study, Plainview
Cruisin' USA, Plano
Themed Entertainment Complex, Rockwall
Sunset Over Texas, Round Rock
Wet Zone Water Park, Rowlett
Neff's Amusement Park, San Angelo
Ingram Park Mall, San Antonio
Remember the Alamo, San Antonio
Missions Resort Park, San Antonio
Water Space Park, San Antonio
San Benito Hotel and Civic Center, San Benito
Aquarena Springs, San Marcos
Kidd-Key Theater, Sherman
Sherman Tourism Study, Sherman
Jeremiah's Waterslide, South Padre Island
Texas Country, Waco
Waco Water Theme Park, Waco

Utah
Lagoon, Farmington

Lagoon A Beach, Farmington
The Point, Sandy
Park City Coal Mine Adventure, Park City
Coal Mine Attraction, Carbon County
BuggyTowne, Brigham City
Festival of the American West, Logan
Utah State Fair, Salt Lake City
World Cinemax, Salt Lake City
Utah Land Development, Salt Lake City

Virginia
Dry Gulch Junction, Wytheville
Central Park Project, Fredericksburg

Washington
Riverfront Park, Spokane
State Fair Project, Spokane
Spokane Coliseum, Spokane
Tumwater Historical Park, Olympia
Fun Forest Seattle Center, Seattle
Water Works, Bellevue
Water Works, Richland

Washington, D.C.
Marriott Corp.

West Virginia
Equestrian Center, Chaplin Hill
Exhibition Park, Morgantown

Wisconsin
Carousel Park, Oshkosh
Wilderness Hotel & Golf Resort, Wisconsin Dells

Enchanted Forest, Wisconsin Dells
Fort Dells, Wisconsin Dells
Mystic Lake, Wisconsin Dells
Riverview Park, Wisconsin Dells
Village Square, Wisconsin Dells
Neesh-la Indian Corporation, Wisconsin Dells
Riverview Boat Lines, Wisconsin Dells
The Haunted Mansion, Wisconsin Dells
Fond du Lac Theme Park, Fond du Lac
National Bowling Hall of Fame, Greendale

West Virginia
Chaplin Hill Equestrian Center, Morgantown

Musical Theatre Glossary

Actor: Someone who portrays a character in a show. In musicals, actors must be "triple-threats": they should be able to sing, dance, and act.

Assistant: Most of the creative staff, i.e., the director and the designers, have assistants to write down their thoughts and notes for future reference. And to get them coffee!

Audience: The most important part of the theatre "team," the audience watches and reacts to the theatrical presentation.

Ballad: A romantic, gracefully flowing song.

Belt: To forcefully sing in almost a shouting tone.

Book: The spoken dialogue between songs in a musical.

Book Writer: The playwright who writes the "book" of a musical.

Cast: The company of actors who perform a play or musical.

Choreographer: The artist who creates the dance and movement of a musical or play.

Company Manager: In charge of the cast's payment and lodgings during a tour of a show.

Composer: The artist who writes the music in a musical.

Costume Designer: Working with the interpretation of the director, the costume designer creates the look of the clothing for each character in a show.

Curtain Call: After the show is completed, the cast comes on stage and bows in front of the audience, accepting the audience's applause. This is the time to really go wild with applauding if you liked the show!

Director: If a show is a ship, then the director is the captain, the artist who interprets the story of the show, telling the actors how to move, how to say their lines and sing their songs. The director usually sets the look of the show with the different designers.

House Manager: In charge of everything in the theatre in front of the stage; that is, in the auditorium of the theatre, or in the "house."

Intermission: The short break in the middle of the show. Take this time to buy some souvenirs, read your program, or use the restroom!

Libretto: The script of a musical.

Lighting Designer: The artist who works with electric lighting instruments to create the atmosphere of the show through light and shadow.

Lyricist: The lyricist writes the words to go along with the composer's music.

Musical Director: The artist in charge of the musical sound of the show. The musical director is often the conductor of the musical.

Orchestra: The collection of musicians who work together to play the music of the show.

Pit: The area where the orchestra plays. The pit is usually just under the front lip of the stage. Check out the orchestra pit during the intermission!

Props: The physical objects used throughout the show. The person in charge of props is called a (drum roll, please!) props person!

Rehearsal: Going over the play again and again before performing to the public.

Set Designer: The artist who designs the physical architecture of the show. The set designer creates the physical world of the story.

Stage Crew: The stage staff who move props and sets during the show.

Stage Manager: In charge of the stage crew, the stage manager also "calls" the show, speaking by microphone to each member of the stage staff, giving cues for lighting, sound, and music.

Swing: An understudy who is able to jump in at a moment's notice and take over many different roles in a show.

Understudy: If an actor gets sick or hurt, the understudy takes over, sometimes at a moment's notice!

Index

—A—
Abominable Showman, The,
  141
Abu Dhabi, 118, 121
Adam's Mark Hotel, 151
Aida, 172
Al Biernat's, 88-89
Albee, Edward, 116
Albers, Josef, 183
Albuquerque, 109, 110
Alton Towers, 122
American Airlines Arena, 45
American Airlines, 114, 151
American Express, 104
Anders, John, ix
Ann-Margret, 93
Apapa, Nigeria, 103
Apapa Park, 101
Aqua Park, 120, 121
Arlington, Texas, 4
Asheville, North Carolina, 183
Atlanta, 65, 67
Australia, 153, 154-160

—B—
Barnum, P. T., 143
Baylor Hospital, 171

Baylor University, 4, 22
Benson, Jodi, 90
Benson's Wild Animal Farm,
  180, 184, 185
Beth, Wanda, ix, 123, 127, 128
Big River, 8
Brady Bunch, The, 85
Bribie Island, Queensland,
  Australia, 159
Brioni, 151
Broadway, 141, 151
Broadway Contemporary Series,
  8, 10
Broome, John, 122-123
Brown, Joe E., 79
Bryant, Helen, ix
Bush, George H. W., 128

—C—
Cagle, Jenny, ix, 128
Cancun, 127
Canon City, Colorado, 189
Caracas, Venezuela, 140
Carnival, 122-123
Carter, Jimmy, 68
Casey, Al, 151
Cats, 167

Centrepoint, 156
Channing, Carol, 76-77
Charleston, South Carolina, 115
Charlotte, North Carolina, 115
Chattanooga, Tennessee, 63
Chattanooga Visitor and
  Convention Bureau, 63
Chevalier, Maurice, 2-3
China, 47-60, 144
Cinderella, 38-40, 78, 178
Clark, Luther D., 195
Clear Channel Entertainment,
  142
Clinton, Bill, 68-69
Coming to the Lord, 42
Cooper, Kenneth, Dr., 49-50
Cotton Bowl, 1, 19, 20
Crandall, Bob, 114
Crow, Margaret, 127, 129-130
Crow, Trammell, 127-128, 129-
  130, 195
Crystal Terrace, 32
Cundy, Doug, 125-127
Curran, Charles, 156
Curtis, Jill, 79, 82
Curtis, Tony, 79-83, 91-92

—D—
Dallas, Texas, 32, 127
Dallas Business Committee for
  the Arts, 151
Dallas Summer Musicals, 2, 6-
  11, 19, 27, 31-36, 38, 76-
  92, 142, 150, 163, 167,
  169, 172, 195
Dallas Summer Musicals School
  of Musical Theatre, 147,
  150-151
Dallas Symphony, 20
Dame Edna, 88, 89
Detroit, Michigan, 186-188
Devil's Going to Get You, The, 42
Diller, Phyllis, 78
Disney, Roy, 90
Disney, Walt, 4, 88

Dragon Lake Park, 47-60
Dubai, 132

—E—
Engel, Georgia, 38-40
English, Lila Grace, iii, 14, 30,
  195, 198
Evita, 172

—F—
Fayetteville, Arkansas, 74-75
Feld, Bonnie, 45
Feld, Kenneth, 45
"Felix the Cat," 17-18
Flower Drum Song, 8, 9

—G—
Galveston, Texas, 127
Genting-Highlands mountains,
  137
Georgetown, Texas, 116
Georgia Governor's Conference
  on Tourism, 67
Goldstein, Col, 157
Goldstein, Hal, 157
Gone With the Wind, 59, 60
Grand Canyon, 112
Grease, 145
Guangzhou, China, 55

—H—
Hassanein, Salah, 94
Hawaiian Islands, 139
Hedger, Albert, 159
Hello Dolly, 76
Hilsabeck, Rick, 83-85
Hong Kong, 58
Hot Springs, Arkansas, 68-69
*How to Succeed in Business
  Without Really Trying*, 176
Hughes, Tom, 2, 6, 27
Humphries, Barry, 88-89

—I—
Ikoyi, Nigeria, 103

Inner Space Caverns, 116
International Association of
   Amusement Parks and
   Attractions (IAAPA), 65

—J—
Japan, 124
Jenkins, Angus, iii, 5, 13, 36,
   69, 105, 195
Jenkins, Berniece, iii, 4, 13, 29,
   46, 148-149
Jenkins, Delanie, iii, 14, 195
Jenkins, Tiffany, 13, 14, 156,
   195
Jenkins, Wendell H., iii
Jenkins, Wendy, iii, ix, 12, 13,
   50, 82-83, 87, 94, 197
Jones, Tom, 40-41

—K—
Kansas City Starlight Theatre,
   38-40
Keflavik, Iceland, 136
Kentucky Fair and Exposition
   Center, 188
Kentucky Kingdom, 188
King and I, The, 8, 87, 141
Kitt, Eartha, 39, 178
Kreisler, Fritz, 20
Krofft, Marty, 41
Kuala Lumpur, Malaysia, 137
Kuwait, 117-118, 120, 121

—L—
Lady Jane Beach, 155
Lagos, Nigeria, 97, 101, 103,
   104
Lake Powell, 112
Las Vegas, Nevada, 72, 109
Leisure and Recreation Concepts
   (LARC), 4, 5, 12, 29, 45, 47-
   60, 68, 116, 118, 124, 133,
   135-137, 140, 144, 153,
   157, 188, 189, 190, 212-
   240

Leno, Jay, 197
Lewis, Jerry, 7
Lida Hooe Elementary School, 15
Lim Tuck Sing, 137-138
Lim Tuck Fatt, 137-138
Lincoln Tunnel, 64
Little Mermaid, 90
Little, Rich, 93
Logan International Airport, 184
Luna Park, 161, 162
Lyn, Bee, 102-103

—M—
Madras, India, 140
Maioris, 139
Majestic Theatre, 8, 10, 41-42,
   156
Malaysia, 137-138
Mansion on Turtle Creek, 82
Marineland, 134
Meeker, Charles, 2, 19, 20, 27
Merrick, David, 141-143
Messilla Beach, 117-118
Mills, Hayley, 87-88
Miss Saigon, 9
Mitchell, Johnny, 72, 73-74
Monrovia, Liberia, 192
Moorea, 130
Mordecai, Benjamin, 9
Mount Daisen, 124
Murchison, Lupe, 189, 190
Murphy, Donna, 142
Music Hall at Fair Park, 1, 3, 7,
   12, 19, 20, 27, 31-36, 37,
   83, 85, 89, 145, 163-179
Music Man, The, 85

—N—
Nashua, New Hampshire, 180,
   184
Nederlander, Jimmy, vi, vii-viii
New York World's Fair, 64
New York Times, The, 143
New York City, 64, 69-70, 72
New Zealand, 139

Newsweek, 169
Niagara Falls, 134, 135
Nigeria, 95-105
Nixon, Richard, 47, 59
Norville, Deborah, 94

—O, P—
Oak Cliff, 15
Papeete, 130
Park Lane Hotel, 70
Peddler Bay, 133
Perth, Australia, 158
Phantom of the Opera, The, 83, 163, 174, 177
Phillips, Lou Diamond, 141
Pied Piper, The, 15
Playcenter, 136-137
Pollard, Dora L., iii
Pollard, Lucille D., iii
Producers, The, 8
Provencher, Arthur, 180, 184-186

—Q—
Queensland, Australia, 159
Quinn, Pat, 41

—R—
Ragtime, 149
Ringling Bros. & Barnum and Bailey Circus, 45-46
Ringling, John, 45
Rio de Janeiro, 122-123
Riverdance, 149-150, 175
Rock City, 63
Rockettes, 196
Rose, Harriet, 168
Royal Gorge Bridge, 189-191

—S—
Saffron, Abe, 157-158
SamaWorld, 137
Sao Paulo, Brazil, 136
Sciacca, Sicily, 135-137
Seville, Spain, 26

Shantou, China, 47, 53, 55, 57
Shook, Ron, 49, 153, 157, 158, 159-160, 183-184, 186
Sicily, 135
Sid and Marty Krofft Puppet Factory, 40
Singin' in the Rain, 146
SITAS, 135
Six Flags Over Texas, 4, 23, 24, 26, 40, 90
Solonga, Lea, 9
Some Like It Hot, 79-81, 91
Sound of Music, The, 36-37
South Pacific, 90, 130, 148
Spam cookoff, 83-85
SPCA, 43
St. George Hotel, 125
Stage Door Charley, 31, 36
State Fair of Texas, 3, 83-84, 144
State Theatre, 156
Statue of Liberty, 192-193
Stemmons, John M., 195
Struthers, Sally, 145-146
Subways Are for Sleeping, 143
Sydney, Australia, 153, 155, 156, 161, 162
Sydney Harbor, 155, 157
Sykes, Bob, 68-69

—T—
Tahiti, 130-132
Tennessee Aquarium, 63
Texas Pavilion, 64
Texas Utilities, 37
Thoroughly Modern Millie, 8
Three Broadway Tenors, 151
Tokyo, 111
Tottori Prefecture, 124
Troika Entertainment, 169
Tune, Tommy, 31, 33, 34, 36, 85

—U—
U.S. State Department, 47

United Arab Emirates, 118, 132
University of Arkansas, 75
University of Texas, 75

—V—
Vancouver, British Columbia, 125
Victoria Island, 133-134

—W—
Webber, Andrew Lloyd, 168
White Horse Inn, 180

Wilkin, Miles, 142
Williams, Barry, 85-86
Wilson, Mark, 138
Windholz, Jerry, 65-67
Wizard of Oz, The, 43-45
WonderLand Park, Dubai, 61, 62
World's Fair, 182
WRR Radio, 92
Wynne, Angus G., Jr., 4, 23, 24, 182-183, 195

MICHAEL A. JENKINS is chairman of Dallas-based Leisure and Recreation Concepts, Inc. (LARC), developer of more than 1,000 theme parks and tourist attractions throughout the world, and president and managing director of Dallas Summer Musicals, Inc., with productions at the Music Hall at Fair Park and The Majestic Theatre in downtown Dallas. An investor in numerous Broadway productions, he co-produced the Broadway musical *Flower Drum Song* in 2002, *Brooklyn, the Musical* in 2004, and has many more shows in the works. On those rare occasions when they're not globetrotting, he and his wife, Wendy, live in Dallas.